THE FATHER'S HEART

THE FATHER'S HEART

GOD'S RELENTLESS LOVE FOR HIS DAUGHTERS

Kristie Kerr

Unless otherwise indicated, all Scripture quotations are taken from the Holy Bible, New Living Translation, copyright 1996, 2004. Used by permission of Tyndale House Publishers, Inc., Wheaton, Illinois 60189. All rights reserved.

Scripture taken from the HOLY BIBLE, NEW INTERNATIONAL VERSION®. Copyright © 1973, 1978, 1984 International Bible Society. Used by permission of Zondervan. All rights reserved.

Scripture taken from The Message. Copyright © 1993, 1994, 1995, 1996, 2000, 2001, 2002. Used by permission of NavPress Publishing Group.

ISBN: 978-0-578-02130-0

Printed in the United States of America

1st Printing

Contents

DEDICATION

This book is dedicated to the three fathers in my life:

Dad – I remember many mornings when you would slide a note under my door and on the pages would be the handwritten prayers you had prayed for me that day. Thank you for praying those prayers and thank you for letting me read your loving thoughts towards me--they were indeed a firm place to stand … I love you.

Jeff – From the day I married you, I knew you would be a fantastic father to our children. But watching you step into that role has surpassed any dream I could have ever had--thank you for loving our children … I love you.

Heavenly Father – I have known You for a long time and yet through the process of writing this book, I feel like we just met. Thank you for being my Father ... I love you.

ACKNOWLEDGEMENTS

When I started the process of writing this book, I was expecting our fourth child. When I finished, she was almost two and writing a book with four little kids running around is harder than one would think!

So – first and foremost, I want to thank my sweet, supportive, amazing husband, Jeff, for all the practical ways in which he enabled me to carve out the hours needed to finish this project. And more importantly, the reassurance and encouragement to keep going when it seemed like an unreachable dream. I love you, Baby ... it's your turn now.

To Lucy, Charlie, Betty and Dottie for being patient when Mommy wouldn't share her laptop with you and lost her cool because you inserted a paragraph of zzzzzzzzzzzzzz's in the middle of Chapter 5. You are my life – and being your mother is my greatest joy.

To my family – Mom, Dad, Kate & Rick and the boys, Grandma & Grandpa Pennington and Granny Lane. For listening – reading – editing – encouraging – and supporting me. I love you all so much.

To Pastor Rob and Becca for standing beside me as I have shared the dream for this project with you. Thanks for saying, "Go for it!" I'm not sure I would have done this without your encouragement.

To my girlfriends who have prayed with me, been excited for me and told me to keep going when I wanted to quit – I love you. I am so rich because you are in my world.

To Barb for your friendship, wisdom, and for being willing to tell me the things I need to hear.

To my dear friend, Carol Hollen, who masterfully edited this book for me. Thank you for the immeasurable hours you spent fixing my mistakes. You are a gift in my life.

To Meg – for your mad design skilz!

To my Moms Group friends – When I started leading this group seven years ago, I was not a very good teacher and an even worse writer. But as you shared your lives and let me into your world, I found myself inspired to study more and communicate better so we could make a bigger difference in the lives of the women in our community. This book would have never happened without you. Thanks for growing with me. I love you guys.

CHAPTER 1

JOURNEY TO THE FATHER'S HEART

Names are funny things. I've had the privilege of naming four beautiful people in my life – three girls and one boy. The time and energy I put into choosing a moniker for my kids is actually quite ridiculous - there's a lot of pressure to get it right.

I want it to be original – but I don't want it to be too weird. I want to make sure it sounds good with our last name. You really have to practice shouting the full name out loud as if you were yelling it in discipline to make sure that it works. And I always worry about the origin and meanings of names. I mean, who wants to name their kid something that means "bitter" - who wants to open that can of worms?

I find it so funny how names evolve over time. Our oldest daughter is named Lucy, but we rarely call her "Lucy." We call her "Luce," "Lulu," "Luce Goose," "Goose," "Gooser"… and the list goes on and on. Our four year old, sweet Betty, has been "Bet Bet" for most of her life, Charlie has been

"Chachie," and dear baby sister, Dorothy, is affectionately called "Dorf Dorf" by her siblings.

Names in Biblical times had even more weight to them. In that culture, a person's name was extremely important. It was a glimpse into their character. Names were statements of who someone was and where they came from. They revealed different aspects of a person – from their profession, to their heritage, to their personality.

So, with that in mind, it is so intriguing to me that God gives Himself so many names. He uses countless adjectives to describe His character. One list that I found actually had 625 different names. Then there were lists of God saying, "I am this…." or "the God who…." When I printed it out, it was actually ten pages long … and that was just one source! God calls Himself many things.

And each one of those names gives us a glimpse into a side of His character. Each one shows us a part of who He is and what He is all about. There are so many aspects of His identity and He reveals those different attributes to us in the names He uses to describe Himself.

I have experienced times when God has shown Himself to me as my Savior. He has pursued me as a prince lavishing love on his princess; He has been my friend and companion in times when I was alone and needed to know that there was someone who understood me; He has been my comforter when I was afraid or discouraged. But lately, I've become intrigued by the name that He calls Himself so often in the Bible: Father.

I have to admit that until recently, I've never really

thought about what it means to have God as my Father. And the more I have immersed myself in the topic, the more I realize that I really have a lot of misconceptions and very little understanding of God as my Heavenly Father.

I have come to realize that my first emotion in relation to God the Father is fear. I don't really believe that He is proud of me. So often, I am convinced that I am letting Him down. Something inside me cannot accept that He has a love so deep and strong for me that NOTHING can ever change it.

All these revelations came as a bit of a shock to me. I had no idea that there was this whole side of God that I was avoiding. So I began a journey to figure out where all these misconceptions came from. I wanted to understand why I saw God the Father in the way I did. I wanted to get past the fears and uncertainties that I had accumulated throughout the years, and gain a clear picture of who my Heavenly Father is.

As I tried to unravel this barrier between myself and God, I began to ask a lot of questions. Where did I get these ideas about the Father? Why am I afraid of Him? Where did these pictures in my mind come from?

There certainly is a connection between our experiences with our earthly fathers and how we relate to our Heavenly Father. We take the experiences that we have had as women and daughters, and we create a similar reflection in our relationship with God. That can be great – and that can be not so great. For most of us, it's probably a healthy balance of both.

I grew up in a home with an amazing father who loved God and his family with all of his heart. He was accepting and protective and extremely engaged in my life. And yet I still have issues. The fact that I was so close to my dad made me never want to let him down. I never wanted to mess up and have him be disappointed in me. I was (and still am) deeply driven to perfection and wanting to always do everything right. The desire to please my father has been a huge driving force in my life.

Perhaps my misconceptions were birthed through uninformed teaching I received at the hand of some well-meaning person. Someone out there, intent on convincing me to stay away from sin might have led me to believe there was a limit to the grace of God. Somewhere I accepted the idea that there was a direct link to the amount of serving I do in the church, and the depth of God's love for me. Somehow I allowed myself to think that if I "do more" or "become better," only then God will be proud of who I am.

These ideas show an immaturity in my faith. They reveal areas in which I have not "grown up" spiritually. Just like my children sometimes misunderstand and misinterpret me as a parent, I can have the same reactions to God the Father.

For example, I was recently disciplining one of my children. In the midst of the conversation, she started to get really sassy with me about something I wouldn't let her do. Finally, I sent her to her room for some "cool down time." When I later went to talk to her, was her response; "Oh Mother, thank you soooo much for taking the time to reprimand me for my behavior. I understand that for my benefit, you are instilling in me a respect for authority and a sense of right and wrong. God bless you for investing in my future?" Of course not! I heard, "Why are you being so mean to me! It's not fair! You never let me do anything!! I was just trying to tell you something and you got SOOOO mad at me!"

I have to admit that I see a bit of myself in her childish reaction. I tend to have the same attitude towards God when things aren't going my way. My response demonstrates how much of my faith is still "stuck" in childhood. I haven't looked honestly and maturely at the character of God. Instead, I have retained these immature pictures of Him that do not accurately represent who He is.

I Corinthians 13:11 says, "When I was a child, I spoke and thought and reasoned like a child. But when I grew up, I put away childish things." The misconceptions I have about my heavenly Father are rooted in childish thoughts and reasoning. I realize that it's time for me to "grow up" spiritually and gain a mature understanding of God. It's time for me to put away my childish lens, and instead gain a clearer picture of His intentions and thoughts toward me.

So, what are some of the common misconstrued perceptions we have about God the Father? Why do so many of us fail to connect with Him in that way?

I think that many of us feel like God the Father is a far-off figure. There is an air of formality and inaccessibility that comes to mind. Many of us feel like He is distant and only concerned with affairs much larger than ourselves. The only time He would intervene is when we make a mistake and

His hand of judgment would come to punish us. In my head, I've conjured up images of a huge man sitting on a throne far away with a big stick just waiting to see if we were going to screw things up. Not too involved, mostly just observing. Not too engaged, just monitoring the situation.

It would be easy for us to believe that God is much too busy to deal with us. It would be understandable to think that He has much grander things to tend to than you and me.

The amazing truth is that, indeed, the Lord of all heaven, the Creator of everything, does think of us and care for us. King David had the same thought when he penned these words: "When I look at the night sky and see the work of your fingers – the moon and stars You set in place –what are mere mortals that You should think about them, human beings that You should care for them? (Psalm 8:3-4)

To me, one of the most ironic thoughts in the world is the fact that God, the most powerful being ever, cares for little ol' me. In fact, it says in Luke that he knows how many hairs I have on my head. He is not far off. He is right here with me. He is closely acquainted with my every thought. And it's not out of some sense of obligation or duty, He truly wants to be close to me. Amazing.

Another "stereotype" of God that I have, is that He is someone that doesn't have any interest in a personal relationship with me. For many of us, this is a direct response to our relationship with our earthly fathers. Many of us had fathers who were an authoritative presence in the home, but yet they had very little involvement in our day-to-day activities. They were strong and sturdy, but distant and removed. They never showed affection. They were reluctant with praise. No matter how deep their love for their children was, they didn't know how to express it.

I have heard stories from countless women who express deep regret at the lack of personal relationship that they had with their earthly fathers. Their bonds were superficial and limited. They had such admiration and respect for these men, and yet they never felt like their dads had the time or interest to invest in them. Their deep longing to be known by their dads was left unfulfilled and unsatisfied.

Many of us have taken this experience with our fathers and placed those traits on God. We see Him as an authority, a provider, a disciplinarian, but we cannot see Him as a loving Father who longs to know us. We cannot understand that He wants to be involved in every part of our lives.

I stumbled upon a verse a while ago that absolutely stopped me in my tracks. Psalm 27:8 says, "My heart has heard you say, 'Come and talk with me.' And my heart responds, 'Lord, I am coming.'" I imagine God the Father walking into the room and sitting down on the bed and saying, "Hey, Kristie, tell me about your day." It speaks of His interest in my thoughts and ideas. It reassures me that not only does He want me to come to Him with my requests, but He wants to know my thoughts, ideas and dreams as well.

God wants my relationship with Him to be close and intimate and vulnerable. And in the same vein, He longs for me to know Him, to understand His thoughts and ideas and character. He desires nothing greater than to know you and to be known by you as well.

Lastly, I think of all the women in the world who were hurt deeply by their earthly fathers, and now the idea of God as their Father is absolutely terrifying. They can't seem to grasp the idea of a father who would never fail them. Many of us are carrying around deep wounds and unhealed hurts that were inflicted at the hand of a parent or other authority figure and therefore the idea of God as a Father brings nothing but fear and skepticism.

I was recently reading an article about the song written by a sixteen-year-old Kelly Clarkson called, "Because of You." Traumatized by the divorce of her parents and the dismantling of her family, she wrote the words, "Because of you I find it hard to trust not only me, but everyone around me." The security and stability that should have been found in her home was shattered by circumstances beyond her control.

The amount of people in this world who have had their lives turned upside down by selfish choices that others have made is staggering. And for many, they cannot fathom a God who never leaves. They cannot imagine a father who doesn't hurt or abuse. Their attempts to trust God are held hostage by fear that He will not follow through with His promises to them.

But Psalm 27:10 tells us "Even if my father and mother abandon me, the Lord will hold me close." I love that God addresses those who have been hurt, abandoned, abused and mistreated by earthly parents. I love the fact that He takes the time to say, "This may have happened to you, but I will hold you close and never let you go."

I know that there is great healing to be found in the arms of our Father. No matter how you have been failed or wounded, He is able to fill that void and the longing in your heart to be a cherished daughter.

All of these ideas can play into our veiled perceptions of who God really is. We take these experiences and ideas, and we form an assessment of who God is. We see thorough a distorted lens; it's not accurate or authentic.

But as I have begun to look honestly at the heart of the Father, something is changing in me. Slowly, He has been revealing to me that this is a side of Him that He wants to show me. That the next step on my journey of faith is to make peace with God my Father. To grab hold of who He is – and let go of who He isn't. The thought of God as my Father should bring me security and peace, not fear and disappointment. So, my prayer has become, "*Show me your Father's heart.*"

I have begun to watch my husband with our daughters. I have begun to notice the way that he deals with them. The things concerning them that are important to him. Surprisingly, there are many things that are important to him, that I have never really considered. A father's heart is very different from a mother's.

He has a different way of dealing with them – a different dynamic, a different understanding of them, a different perspective. I worry about their safety, but protecting them is at whole different level for him. Providing for their needs is huge for him – making sure that they are taken care of and provided for.

He loves to see them try new things, and admires their courage, where I'd just rather keep them close by where I know they won't get hurt. I remember a couple of years ago when I registered Lucy for our community baseball league. Unfortunately, in all my administrative genius, I registered her for the boys' league instead of the girls'. When she and Jeff showed up for their first practice, they stumbled upon my error. The coach said she was welcome to practice with them, and then sign up for the girls' team the following week. Jeff asked Lucy what she wanted to do, and after a moment of apprehension, she decided she wanted to play with the boys.

Now, there's a huge difference between first grade boys playing ball, and first grade girls. The girls are chatty and giggly, whereas the boys are all about how hard and fast they can throw the ball to each other. But my sweet girl jumped out there and played catch and shagged fly balls with the guys.

When Jeff brought her home that night, he was absolutely glowing. He had taken a whole roll of pictures of her and was as proud as I've ever seen him. I, of course, was mortified that he let our little angel play with the rough boys, but Jeff's buttons were bursting. He said, "To see her be afraid of something and do it anyway, was amazing. Nothing gets to me more than seeing our kids be brave."

Each of these fatherly qualities has opened a door to understanding God's heart toward me. Through the eyes of the good and loving earthly fathers around me, I have begun to catch a glimpse of the attributes that my Father in heaven wants to reveal to me.

But more than any other trait I have observed in Jeff toward our kids, I am absolutely struck by his love for them. Purely unabashed, unconditional, in-total-awe kind of love. There is a warmth in the love of a father that doesn't compare with any other type of love I've seen. A genuine affection that supercedes romantic love. A heartfelt pride that is distinct from maternal love. A love that can give you a firm place to stand on with confidence and strength.

A couple of years ago, my oldest daughter had her 6th birthday party. She had a "dance" party and we pulled out all the stops with moving lights and a DJ. In the middle of the night, a slow song came on, and I watched my daughter melt into the arms of her father for a "daddy-daughter" dance. She buried her head in his chest and immersed herself in the sweetest dance. She suddenly ignored the room full of screaming girls who had come to celebrate her, and her expression completely changed. She had no other desire than to be in his arms. Totally safe, totally accepted, totally confident in his love for her.

I have thought of that moment many times. But recently, I've taken the time to remember not my daughter's face, but the face of my husband. His expression matched hers completely. As much as she wanted to be with him, he wanted nothing more than to be with her.

That's a Father's heart. That's the heart of MY Father towards me.

I want to clearly see my Father's heart. I want to understand what He is thinking of when He looks at me. I want to believe in His acceptance of me. I don't want to be afraid of the hand of my Father any more.

I want to see His face while He dances with me.

CHAPTER 2

TRUSTING THE FATHER'S HEART

Why is it that I have such a hard time trusting God? Just when I think I have a handle on it, something comes up that rocks my world and I think, "I don't understand You at all!" A dear friend who is an incredibly godly woman with five children is diagnosed with brain cancer. A friend whom I loved and respected has a moral failure and I hold his wife's hand as she wonders how she can possibly survive the betrayal. I watch a couple long for another child only to suffer another miscarriage and another blow to their faith.

Maybe it's the idealist in me. I truly believe that God is all powerful. Nothing is too big for Him. He can do anything – and there is nothing that He can't do. That's not the part with which I struggle. What I struggle with is this ... "If God can do anything, why doesn't He just fix it all?" Why would He allow us to go through all the pain and disappointment? If He has the ability to get us out of these horrible situations, wouldn't a loving father just do it?

Everytime. No exceptions. No wondering if it's His plan or will … just a blanket "get out of jail free" card.

Idealist or not, the truth is that bad things do indeed happen. People get sick; people die; people hurt us; things don't always work out the way we think they should. In my heart, I want to trust God, but the reality of the circumstances of life cause me to doubt.

Our son was born 12 weeks prematurely. When he was about five days old, he developed a severe lung complication. As Jeff and I sat in a small room in front of Charlie's chest x-rays, we heard the words every parent fears, "There's nothing more we can do for him." As we got in the car and headed home, I remember saying to my husband, "I am completely confident that God can heal Charlie. I just know that sometimes He chooses not to. And I am terrified that this time, He isn't going to heal him."

Amazingly and miraculously, God did heal our little boy. And not a night goes by when I tuck him into bed, that I don't whisper, "Thank you, Jesus."

But what if He hadn't? What if He had something else in mind? What if all the days ordained for Charlie's life were only five days long, and His plan involved us losing our precious little boy?

These are the questions that haunt me. And these are the questions that reveal the deepest uncertainties of my faith. Is my walk with Jesus simply about avoiding pain? Is He simply my "supernatural security blanket" who will never allow anything to happen to me or anyone I care about? If something bad happens, is it a lapse in His care for me?

How can a loving Father sit by and watch His children suffer? Can I really trust Him?

Deep down, I have a preconceived notion that a loving Father would not allow his children to be hurt. He would stop all suffering, sickness and disaster at the door ... "No way, you're not getting to MY kid!"

Maybe that's part of the mother in me. As a mother, I am constantly in "prevention" mode. I am forever watching for anything that could cause the slightest pain or injury; I read every article about every possible danger. My greatest goal is to keep them from experiencing anything that would make them sad or confused or disappointed. I try and think of every possible scenario that could bring them any kind of discomfort and want to do everything to keep them out of the situation.

But Jeff's perspective is completely different. He's less concerned with their immediate comfort, and is more concerned with their "character training." He makes them wait a while before he gives them what they're asking for. He makes them leave their favorite toy at home instead of lugging it around town. If they become too set in their ways, he instinctively wants to find a way to break them of their habits. The father in him is more interested in teaching them how to grow *through* the situations they might face.

Lately we've been dealing with Charlie not wanting to ride his bike. He got a brand new bike this summer, a shiny red Hot Wheels two wheeler with training wheels. We brought the bike home and Jeff proceeded to take the kids out for a ride to the park. As they headed down the road, Charlie got a little off balance and fell headfirst off of his new bike. His helmet took the brunt of the fall, but he scraped up his face and hands. It was a traumatic moment for the boy.

Ever since then Charlie has wanted nothing to do with his bike. Every evening after dinner, Jeff says, "Okay Charlie, time for a bike ride." Charlie's little lip starts quivering and he says, "But I don't WANT to go on a bike ride. I'm going to fall!" So, what does Mom say? "That's okay son, you don't have to get on that scary bike anymore!" But Dad, on the other hand, says, "Sorry, but you're going." See, while I'm more concerned about Charlie's immediate fear of falling, Jeff is more concerned about Charlie getting over his fear and becoming a kid that loves to ride around on his bike.

So, I'm wondering - is God more concerned about my "immediate comfort", or is He more interested in my "character training?" What if, by allowing me to experience trials and heartache, He is preparing me for something greater. What if He is allowing my friend's cancer to demonstrate some higher purpose through her life? I know that God has taught her and her family so much through this sickness. I know she has clung to Jesus in a way that is unfathomable to those who haven't been through such a situation.

What if my friend's struggle with her husband's sin is leading toward a ministry and closer relationship with Christ and each other than they could've ever imagined? What if the pain of having the sin brought into the light would pale in comparison to the devastation that would've occurred if their path went along unchallenged and unchanged? I have watched as they have dug in and repaired a marriage that some would have sworn was not worth saving. And they look at each other differently now. There is an intimacy in their eyes that shows a depth I had never seen before. Now they know what they're fighting for.

What if my friend's struggle for a baby is simply a step on a road to something greater? Next week she is meeting with an adoption agency. Could it be that God allowed her to long for a child for so many years to bring her to the place where she was willing to adopt? Is there some child somewhere that God has, in His universal design, planned to be raised in this Christian home and this was the road He chose to bring her there?

I'm reminded of the story of Hannah in the Bible. She too, longed for a child for many years. She was taunted by others and tortured by her inability to conceive. Finally, she made a vow to God. She said, "O Lord Almighty, if you will look down upon my sorrow and answer my prayer and give me a son, then I will give him back to you. He will be yours for his entire lifetime." (I Samuel 1:11)

She vowed that if she was granted a son, that she would take him to the temple to be raised by Eli so that he would know the scriptures and the ways of the Lord. God granted her request and the child born to her was Samuel. The one who helped lead the wayward children of Israel back to God. The one who anointed Saul as king. The one who was a spiritual father to David ... the man after God's own heart.

Do you think Samuel would've been the spiritual leader he was if he hadn't grown up in the temple? Would he have heard so clearly from God if he hadn't had the daily mentorship of Eli? And would Hannah had ever made the vow to give him (literally) to the work of the Lord if she hadn't come to that point of desperation after her years of pain? Could it be that the very essence of God's plan for bringing Israel back to Himself began with the heartache of one lonely woman and her longing for a child?

My human, mommy heart says that God shouldn't have allowed Hannah all that pain. The compassion in me wishes that no one would ever suffer such heartache. But that's not the promise God gives us. Actually, the promise God gives is something quite different. God says that we WILL face troubles in this life. John 16:33 says, "Here on this earth you will have many trials and sorrows." Why?

First of all, we live in a sinful world. The Garden of Eden was perfect. There was no sin, no sickness, no death. But when sin entered the scope of mankind, suddenly the rules were changed. From that moment on, there was heartache and sorrow. Our human bodies are imperfect, they get sick and we all eventually die.

Secondly, because of sin, people make choices that affect our lives. Someone could choose to drink and drive and run into my car. Their sinful choices affect me. We all must at one time or another, face painful circumstances which were a result of someone else's sin and poor choices.

And we're not off the hook ourselves either! Just as easily as we can be hurt by someone else's choices, many times we are our own worst enemies. We make bad choices, say stupid things, and selfishly walk down the wrong path. It's hard to admit it while you in the middle of the heartache, but a lot of our problems are of our own making.

So, it's true, we face hardship because we live in a sinful and fallen world. But back to my original point, why doesn't God just fix it all? If He has the ability to make all that pain go away, why does He sometimes choose to let us walk through it instead of taking it away?

First of all, we need to remember that God has given each one of us free will. He allows us to make our own decisions and choices; He gives us the freedom to choose Him or reject Him.

In the same way, if God imposed His will on everyone else's choices – just to keep me from having to face unpleasant circumstances – that would not line up at all with His character. It would be like a woman I once knew who was so protective of her kids that she never allowed them to go anywhere. They were home schooled, weren't allowed in the church nursery or kids programs, and had no friends outside their home. One day she told me, "I'm so excited, I found a college home school curriculum. Now the kids can even go to college at home!"

Was her approach helping them or hurting them? In what way was she preparing them to face the world? If they never had to face anything, how were they to grow and develop wisdom and discernment? God could protect us by restricting all our choices and experiences, but then how could we ever choose to make Him our personal Savior? Free will opens the door to both good and bad decisions. But that is what God does - He gives us the choice.

As much as I think that God should just place us all in a little bubble of safety, I recognize that His ultimate purpose is not about my personal comfort. Just as my husband is concerned about Charlie growing and overcoming the fear he has for his bike, God the Father is interested in helping me grow. His plan is to shape me into His very image. His desire is that I would become more and more full of Christ — and less and less of Kristie.

Romans 5:3 says, "We can rejoice, too, when we run into problems and trials, for we know that they are good for us — they help us learn to endure. And endurance develops strength of character in us, and character strengthens our confident expectation of salvation."

Some of you are just like my Charlie: You are holding on with white knuckles screaming, "I don't like this!" And God the Father is running alongside saying, "If you just trust Me, pretty soon you will understand why I made you go through this." He is teaching you to endure; He is producing strength and character in you; He's teaching you to ride your bike.

And just as He longs to see you personally grow, there is a much grander picture at stake. You see, there is a plan so much greater than you and I can even imagine, and we are a part of it. His plan is to seek and save the lost; His plan is to bring the hurting and wounded to him; His plan is to draw all men to Himself ... and you are to play a part in that master plan.

I recently was asked by a friend to pray for a little girl who was an acquaintance of hers who had been diagnosed with neuroblastoma, a rare form of cancer. I decided to check out her Web page to watch her progress and began reading her father's daily entries and updates.

I could hardly bear to read the words of this brokenhearted man and look at the photos of this beautiful two-year-old girl. For you see, a few months prior to this, I had become overcome with the fear that something bad could happen to one of my children. For some reason, that seed had grabbed a hold of me, and my stomach was in knots. I wanted a guarantee. I wanted God to promise me that nothing would ever happen to them. When I realized that this kind of assurance would never come, I became more and more upset with God.

As I read each day, the words of a father who was facing the most horrific thing that I could ever imagine, I was absolutely moved by his faith. He shared how God was showing him the story of Abraham and how he was asked to give up his only son. This father grappled with the thought of losing his only daughter and questioning how God could allow such a thing to happen.

His words struck me to the core. After arguing, and yelling, and screaming with God, he eventually came to the conclusion that this baby girl was not his – but God's. And he trusted God with whatever He had planned. This was not the stubborn resignation of a man who had lost hope, but the quiet peace that comes from finally understanding the true heart of the Father and confidence that comes through that realization.

As this stranger allowed me to silently observe his journey, something inside me came to rest as well. I, too, could trust the hand of my Father even if faced with something so horrific. If he could place his daughter in God's sovereign hands, then I could as well.

I'm sure there are grander ways that God used this sweet family that I have never met, but they changed my life. God used a vulnerable heart, open and honest to Him, to speak to my fearful spirit; in a small way, God's heart for me was revealed through the pen of a stranger.

The power of your testimony can reach a lost soul. The witness of your strength in a storm can inspire the weakest of hearts. Your faith in the face of a trial can shout volumes to a world that has nothing to believe in. God will use your victories and defeats, your questions and answers, your fears and bravery to show Himself to the world; but we have to be willing to let Him.

It all boils down to this: Do I trust God with my life? I admit that in the past, my definition of trusting God meant believing that God would never let anything bad happen to me or the people I love. And the reality that bad things do indeed happen put a big question mark right in the middle of my attempts to trust God. But I've begun to realize that when I say that I trust God with my life, I have to say that I trust Him not only to protect me, (which He does) and to heal me, (which He has). I must be able to say, "I trust that if you allow me to go through something painful, that You will be with me through the entire thing." You will be there. You will be in the pain, and confusion, and frustration. You will comfort me when I don't understand what is going on. You will give me strength when I think I can't take another step. You will give me the grace to take whatever I may face and use it to further Your Kingdom.

Jesus was the perfect example of this. When He was in the Garden of Gethsemane, hours away from being crucified, I believe that Jesus had a "Do I Trust You?" moment. The Bible says He became overwhelmed at the prospect of what He was going to face. Mark 14:36 says that He fell onto the ground and said, "Abba, Father, everything is possible for you. Please take this cup of suffering away from me."

This sounds a little bit like my bargaining with my Heavenly Father. "God, I know you are able to do anything, please keep anything from ever happening to me or my family." But Jesus' next words show that He truly understood His purpose - "Yet, I want to do your will, not mine."

In my own heart, I must come to the point where I can say, "I may think I know how everything should go, but I recognize, God, that you have a plan and more than anything I want to do Your will."

To say this wholeheartedly, I must let go of my idealistic notions about God and my purpose for making Him my Lord and Savior. Am I in this thing just to have a perfect, pain-free life? Am I following God simply to enhance my earthly experience? Or do I have an eternal perspective; able to see the grander picture of what God has for my life?

In Mark 6, there is a story about Jesus and the disciples on a boat in the middle of a great storm. The disciples were terrified, and woke Jesus up in a frantic panic. The words He spoke to them are the word He has spoken to me as I realize there may be countless storms through which I will need to trust my Father's heart - He said three things: "It's all right; I am here; don't be afraid."

My prayer is that I would continue to grow in my trust of God my Father. That I would let go of the fear that something bad could happen, and instead place my trust in the fact that no matter what I may face, my Heavenly Father is right there next to me and will carry me through whatever comes my way.

CHAPTER 3

THE FATHER'S ACCEPTANCE

I was watching a talk show one day, and there was a girl on who was struggling with her weight. Her self-esteem was at an all time low and she was considering drastic surgery to help her finally lose the pounds. As they discussed the issue further, the subject of her father came up. He was constantly on her case about what she was eating and how much she was exercising. He was also a guest on the show, and he said that he was merely concerned about her and was trying to help. She constantly felt like she could never measure up to what he thought she should be. In a vicious cycle, the more she ate, the more she felt like he disapproved of her. And the more she felt his disapproval, the more she wanted to eat – and the more he vocalized his concerns about her weight. I remember feeling sorry for the girl. You could see in her eyes that she so desperately just wanted to have her father's approval and acceptance, but she felt like he couldn't love her unless she lived up to his expectations for how she looked.

I was recently talking to a friend who was really struggling with her self worth. She also had grown up in a house where her weight and appearance were items to joke about and topics of which to make fun. She said, "I know that a lot of my issues are connected to things that my dad said to me that I just can't get past."

And the truth of the matter is, all of us in one way or another has had to face rejection and feeling like we just don't measure up. Perhaps your parents were uninterested, or absent, or insensitive, or any other list of things that left a wound on the heart of their little girls. There are wives who struggle daily in a loveless marriage where they are neither seen nor heard - just ignored. Young girls who worked and worked to make the team, or get the job, or be a part of the clique, only to face the exclusion of unacceptance.

Many of us are walking around with this inner voice nagging in our heads saying, "You're just not good enough." We feel like we can never quite become the person we were meant to be; never live up to the standard set by those around us; never quite get over the hurdle.

The hurt from feeling rejected affects us all in different ways. While it causes some to retreat into a shell of fear and avoidance, it propels others into a frantic ambition for perfection. Some of us face the inner voice head on and set out to prove it wrong by achievement and success, and others collapse under its weight and begin to self-destruct.

Perhaps your rejection has affected how you feel about your appearance. Maybe you constantly look in the mirror and think, "Nope, not quite right." Maybe something in you always feels like you are too fat or too skinny or too short or too tall. Your hair's the wrong color or your skin is the wrong shade or your nose is the wrong shape.

Maybe it's about your abilities. Maybe you never quite feel like you've done a good enough job. Maybe you can never work enough hours to satisfy the drive inside you. Maybe your house can never be clean enough. Or, maybe you never would consider applying for that promotion – because "I'm sure that there's someone better out there than me." Maybe you have kept all your dreams for success and the future locked away deep in your heart because you've never felt the confidence to take a risk and try something new.

Or maybe you are paralyzed when it comes to relationships. You may keep everyone at arm's length, because you fear that if they get to know the real you, they will reject you. Maybe you constantly test those who love you just to make sure that they will stick around. And instead of growing healthy relationships – you are in a constant cycle of neediness.

Before I met my husband, I was in a serious relationship with a boy for a couple of years. He told me he loved me. He told me he wanted to marry me. And then one day, he just walked away. I never saw it coming. He said that he just wasn't ready for all of it; I could accept that. It was about him, not me - right? That is until a few months later when I heard that he was engaged to someone else. Ouch. The truth was – it WAS me! He was perfectly ready to marry this other girl. There was no fear of committing to her. I was forced to recognize that he wasn't afraid to get married, he just didn't want to marry me, and that was a tough pill to swallow. I became so self-conscious, suspicious and untrusting that I could barely function. The wound of offering yourself to someone, only to have them say, "Thanks, but no thanks" is deep.

And all the baggage that we carry around from the rejection at the hands of others in our lives can affect our relationship with God. Many times I feel like I have let Him down. I feel like I don't measure up to what He wants me to be. I feel like I have failed Him by not doing more, or being better, or sinning less.

I remember meeting a girl in college who just seemed to have it all together when it came to her relationship with God. She seemed so content and peaceful. She always seemed to hear from God and enjoy such a close relationship with Jesus.

Then there was me. I could never quite figure out what God wanted me to do. I felt my relationship with Jesus was more of a guessing game than anything else. I constantly struggled with hearing His voice and following through with the things I thought He wanted me to do. And the more I prayed and tried to become more "spiritual," the more I felt like I was missing the mark.

I was convinced that Jesus loved her more than he loved me, that the special relationship that my friend had with God was exclusive. She was in the "Jesus Cool Kids Club," and I was forever to remain an outsider with my face pressed against the glass. I could try as hard as I wanted, but God had "chosen" her and rejected me.

And for some of you, that feeling of being unacceptable to God goes even deeper. You have royally screwed up; you have made a big mistake; you have done things that you never thought you would ever do. And you are convinced that from now on, you are "off the list" when it comes to God.

So, is that the truth? Is our Heavenly Father like the guy on the talk show who is just interested in telling us all the things we've done wrong so we can "get our act together?" Is it true that God really "chose" my friend and just tolerated me? Have you really gone too far for God to ever accept you?

I think because we have experienced so much rejection in our lives, it's hard for us to not expect the same response from God. Especially if you've faced rejection at the hand of someone close to you, whom you trusted and who was supposed to care for you - it makes sense that you would expect the same conditional love from your Heavenly Father.

But Isaiah 55:8-9 tells us a different story. It says, "My thoughts are completely different from yours," says the Lord. "And my ways are far beyond anything you could imagine. For just as the heavens are higher than the earth, so are My ways higher than your ways and My thoughts higher than your thoughts."

God doesn't do things the way we do things. He doesn't have His own baggage like your earthly father that might cause Him to reject or abandon you. He doesn't have the same standard of beauty that the world looks at. He doesn't approach His relationship with you with conditions and standards for achievement to receive His love; God doesn't do things the way we do things.

The truth of God the Father is that His love and acceptance of us is not based on anything we have done or could ever do. He doesn't love you more because you volunteer at church and He doesn't love you less because you struggle with anger or jealousy.

Romans 5:8 says, "But God showed His great love for us by sending Christ to die for us while we were still sinners."

Jesus didn't come to earth to die on the cross for you because you somehow proved that you were worthy of saving. The Bible says that because of His great love for you, He died for you before you even knew you needed a Savior. Later in Romans 5, it says that God died for us while we were still His enemies. God's love for you has nothing to do with your behavior. His acceptance of you is based solely on the fact that He loves you - you didn't earn His sacrifice then, and you don't need to earn it now.

I know that it can be very hard to grasp that kind of grace. We are so used to earning other's affection and approval, that sometimes we just can't get our heads around the idea of someone accepting us no matter what. But in Romans, it says, "Can we boast, then, that we have done anything to be accepted by God? No, because our acquittal is not based on our good deeds. It is based on our faith. So we are made right with God through faith and not obeying the law." (Romans 3:3-4)

A friend of mine was recently sharing a story about her father. This man was a well-respected pastor with three beautiful daughters. For some reason, his youngest daughter began to walk down a path of self-destruction. She had begun to walk in a lifestyle of rebellion and pain. After years of running fast and hard, she finally hit rock bottom. She was addicted to alcohol and drugs, had become a stripper and had slept with countless men. She called her sister and said, "I can't believe what I've become. There is no way that God could ever forgive me." She was tired and she was hopeless.

So what did she do? She called her father. And a few hours later, her dad was on a plane flying to get her to bring her home. I don't know how it all turned out. I'm sure there is a long road ahead of her and many decisions to be made. But I couldn't get past the fact that her father went after her. Here is a man who could've piously judged her; he could have worried more about his position and pride; he could have tried to accentuate his disapproval of her choices by leaving her there in her mess.

But that's not what a father's heart does. A father's heart wants to see his child safe and whole. A father's heart can look past the dirt and grime on the surface, and see his beautiful daughter and all the glory she possesses within her. A father's heart doesn't rub her nose in the wreckage of mistakes and bad decisions, but holds out the potential and dreams that his little girl was meant to achieve. That's what a father's heart does.

There is a beautiful verse in 2 Samuel. It says, "That is why God tries to bring us back when we have been separated from Him. He does not sweep away the lives of those about which He cares – and neither should you." (2 Samuel 14:14) God doesn't give up on us just because we struggle. He never throws up His hands in frustrations and says, "I've had enough … I'm walking away." He does not sweep away the lives of those He cares.

Maybe that kind of father's love seems unfathomable to you. But that's exactly the kind of love that God the Father wants to lavish on you. Yeah, He knows you're not perfect - that's why He sent Jesus to die for you. He knew you were going to make mistakes, so He provided a way for you to be clean before Him so that you could be together again. Yeah, He's going to want you to grow and change and make better choices, but He wants to be there right along side you as you mature. He loves it when you serve Him, but much more than that, He loves you because you are His daughter.

What would happen if you truly believed that God accepts you? Would you stop being so hard on yourself? Would you feel confident enough to try something new? Would you stop being driven to succeed at all costs and realize that you are okay just *being* and not *doing*? Would your approach to relationships change? Would you be so secure in God's acceptance of you, that the un-acceptance of others, while still painful, wouldn't destroy your confidence? Would you be able to say as David did in Psalm 108:1, "My heart is confident in You, O God. No wonder I sing Your praises."?

There is such comfort in resting in the acceptance of God the Father. There is a security that comes from knowing that He loves you no matter what. There is a confidence that comes in knowing that He will always be there for you.

God accepts you. He will never reject you. He doesn't play favorites. He will always be there to help you pick up the pieces. You are accepted by your Father.

CHAPTER 4

THE FATHER'S CHALLENGE

When I was about six years old, my parents signed me up for swimming lessons. I went to the class everyday and learned all about floating, treading water and doing the doggy paddle. After a few months of lessons, it was time to take the test to see if you passed into the next level; I was going to have to demonstrate all of the skills that I had learned. But instead of being in the shallow water, I was going to have to prove myself in the deep end of the pool. As my turn came to go, I got really scared and I refused to get in the water. Refused. My mom still laughs about it to this day. "You just stood there and said, "Nope. I am NOT getting in." I never made it to the next level.

We were just at the pool the other day, and I was watching our daughter, Betty, playing with her dad. Jeff was in the water, and Betty was standing on the edge of the pool, ready to jump in. Jeff had his arms outstretched and kept saying, "Jump in, Betts - I'll catch you!" You could see by her body language that she wanted so badly to jump in. She would lean forward as far as she could and then at the last second, jump back. She even tried making a running leap at it. She would take a few steps back and then start running toward the edge. But just as she would get there, she'd put the brakes on and come to a screeching halt. Finally, she made the leap. She came out of the water with a huge smile on her face. Dad was pretty pumped about it too.

When I see Jeff most excited about our kids, it is when they do something that they were originally afraid to do. He loves to see them rise to the challenge. He is so proud of them when they overcome their reservations and hesitations and try something new - he loves to see them be brave. This is so foreign to me: I am definitely proud of their achievements, but I'd be just as happy if they stayed away from the edge altogether and just stuck with what they know how to do.

That's why God made dads. Where moms like to keep the babes in the nest, dads are the ones who tend to shove the kiddos out; they push them to try new things; they stretch them past the point of what they think they can do.

And I believe that God the Father does the same thing with us. I think He loves to see us step out and do extraordinary things; He wants us to take risks for Him; He wants us to be brave.

In my walk with Jesus, I have always felt God pushing me to do things that I never thought I could do. He has challenged me to take steps of faith that scared me to death. There have been many times that I felt like I was jumping off a cliff. Why does He do that?

There is no doubt that God does miraculous things. Just get five minutes into any book of the Bible, and you will see Him doing the impossible and extraordinary. And although there are times when He just reaches down from heaven and performs a miracle, more often than not He uses a human to accomplish the amazing event. The Red Sea was parted when Moses stretched out his hand. The walls of the city fell down when Joshua and his people raised a shout. The giant fell when David threw the stone ... God uses people to accomplish His work.

And that's where you and I come in: He is still in the business of using His people to accomplish His purposes. Just think of it - He still has plans to reveal Himself to our lost and hurting world; He has plans to further His kingdom on earth; He has plans to do the extraordinary and miraculous ... and His plan involves *you*.

I get so excited when I think about that! Of course I want to be a part of what God is doing; of course I want to see miracles and experience things that could only happen through the moving of His hand; of course I want to be used by Him in any way that I can.

Here's the problem: I get scared. I start running toward the edge of the pool and then suddenly put the brakes on and come to a screeching halt. I stand at the edge hearing my Father say, "Come on Kris, jump in - I'll catch you!" and everything in me leans forward with the anticipation of what wonderful things He has in store, but I just can't seem to make the leap.

What am I afraid of? Well first of all, it seems to me that

more often than not God asks me to do things outside of what I think I'm capable of doing. I feel Him challenge me to go in a direction in which I'm not sure I'm ready to go.

I'm more than willing to do the things with which I'm comfortable; the things in which I feel confident and for which I feel prepared. I'd be happy to oblige in the areas where I have proven myself before and things at which I trust myself to be successful.

I really think a lot of it is a matter of pride: I don't want to look foolish; I don't want to fail; I don't want others to see me vulnerable. The perfectionist in me wants to protect myself from any situation where I don't *know* for sure that I can do it.

I was a vocal performance major in college. I loved to sing and even more, I loved to perform in front of people. If I knew I was singing for something, I used to practice hour upon hour. I would go over every note and every word over and over until I knew I could perform it perfectly. I never wanted to look like I didn't know what I was doing - it was very important to me to always appear polished and together.

Then right after I graduated, I took a job as the music director of a church in North Carolina. The first week I was there, the main piano player quit, so I was the only one who could play for the services. Now, I can play the piano ... but I had never really led worship from the piano. I could read music, but I couldn't just play anything by ear.

My first Sunday, the church was full of people. I had prepared the worship set and practiced over and over again, and was feeling fairly confident about the service. Halfway through the worship time, the pastor got up and said, "Why don't we sing that old hymn together?" I'd tell you what the song was, but I don't remember. I don't remember because I didn't know it. I felt my face get hot and my heart start pounding in my chest. He looked over to me to start playing, and I just froze. I grabbed the hymnbook and started franticly looking for the song. But he couldn't wait, so he just started singing. I started plunking out one note at a time; trying to figure out what key he was in. I tried to play along, but it was a complete and total disaster. I felt like every eye in the place was on me, and I was humiliated. All the energy I had put into *never* being caught unprepared, and in one minute every fear I had came to fruition.

The next week, the same thing happened. And the next service after that. And the next one after that. I actually sat and played through the entire hymnal just to try and be prepared. But that guy *still* managed to start singing a song I didn't know.

It got to the point where I was terrified of getting up on that stage. Every Saturday night I would go to the church and sit in the dark and beg God to not let me be embarrassed again. I couldn't bear to be so vulnerable in front of those people. I hated the fact that they had seen me flawed and imperfect.

The answer I received from God was certainly not the one I wanted; I wanted Him to take me out of the embarrassing situation; I wanted Him to assure me that I would never again be placed in a position where I wasn't comfortable.

Instead, He began to open my eyes that my refusal to be vulnerable was hindering my ministry - I was inaccessible - I was unapproachable. If I was going to make an impact in people's lives, it was going to have to be through being open and transparent with my struggles and shortcomings. My perfect persona was a myth anyway, and it was time to let the cat out of the bag.

God placed me right in the middle of a situation where I couldn't have possibly been more uncomfortable. He had a plan to not only do some great things during my time there; He had a plan to change my heart and motives.

Another reason I get afraid to step out is that it seems so much bigger than what I can handle. He asks me to pray a prayer that I'm not sure will be answered. He asks me to stand up for something that I'm not sure I could defend if need be. He asks me to try something that I feel like there is no way I can accomplish in my own strength.

And that's really the point, right? The reason He asks us to do things that are so much bigger than ourselves, is so that we depend on Him. He wants it blatantly obvious to us and everyone else that it was God who did the miracle.

If there is one lesson I feel like I am continually learning, it's that God wants the glory - He does things to show Himself great – not to show *me* great. I truly believe that He puts me in positions where I need Him to intervene or I will fall flat on my face so that I remember that it is Him who is accomplishing the work.

The times when I have felt inadequate are the times I truly rely on God; I pray harder; I trust greater. I put no confidence in my abilities or preparations – because when faced with the size of the task at hand, they seem futile anyway. If He doesn't show up – it's game over.

Moses was a man who knew that if God didn't intervene, he was going to be in big trouble. When God called him to lead His people, Moses argued all the reasons why he was unqualified, mismatched, and insufficient for the job at hand. But God called him anyway – promising to always be with him. In Exodus 33, God said, "I will personally go with you, Moses, and I will give you rest—everything will be fine for you." (Exodus 33:14 NLT)

And because Moses was so keenly aware of the gap between his ability and the enormity of what God's plan was, he was totally reliant on God to do the work. In Exodus 33:15-16, Moses said, "If you don't personally go with us, don't make us leave this place. How will anyone know that you look favorably on me—on me and on your people—if you don't go with us? For your presence among us sets your people and me apart from all other people on the earth."

I've heard it said that God will never give you more than you can handle. It's a nice sentiment, but I disagree with it. In my life, it seems like God continually gives me more than I can handle. But it's not more than He can handle. So instead of trusting in my own strength and abilities, I throw myself at His mercy and beg Him to show up or I'm sunk! And the beauty of the whole thing is that He *always* shows up, and my faith in Him grows stronger each and every time I see him come through.

Lastly, I think that God challenges us because He wants

to see us grow. The walk of faith that you and I are on is a journey. We should be constantly growing and changing. We shouldn't be doing the same thing today that we were doing five years ago: A healthy relationship with Jesus should include transformation and growth.

Every year we take our kids to the doctor for their "well child visits." Actually, when they're younger, you take them every few months. They check their weight and height and chart out their growth on a graph to make sure they are making progress. Then they ask the parents to fill out a development questionnaire. It covers their speech, fine motor skills, large motor skills, and cognitive development. I always get a kick out of the parents trying to get their kids a high score. "Here Johnny, stand on one foot. Oops, that wasn't long enough … try it again…." Why do they do those tests? To make sure that the kids are progressing in their development. They want to see that they are making strides in all these areas.

Sweet Charlie has always struggled with those tests. Thanks to an early arrival on the planet – and a rough first year of life, he has what the doctors call "developmental delay." It means that he consistently has been a year behind in his developmental milestones - he crawled late - he walked late - he talked late … he just had a lot of catching up to do.

So what have we done to help him? We take him to physical therapy and speech clinicians and occupational therapists. We take him to see the world's most patient women who make him cut with scissors and do sit ups and answer questions. He doesn't like it. He learned early on to say, "This is too hard for me!" But we make him do it anyway - we push him - we insist that he do the work. We make him do it because we know that the more he does the things that are challenging to him, the stronger he will become. And the stronger he becomes, the easier new things will be. What right now might seem frustrating and difficult, will in the end, give him the tools to face the tests that are coming around the corner.

God is pushing you to work on those areas that are frustrating and difficult. Maybe you tried something and failed, so you have determined to never try again; maybe you feel like you kept hitting brick walls, and so you just gave up; maybe you're really comfortable with that behavior or lack of involvement and so you just don't care to take the challenge God is giving you to grow out of that habit or change that area of your life.

You might look at the opportunity in front of you and say, "This is too hard for me." But your Heavenly Father is saying, "You have to do the work - it will help you get stronger. It will take you to the next stage of what it is I have for you; it will get rid of this flaw in your character and it will develop the traits for the next thing I have for you."

God knows your future – where He wants you to be five years from now – and how you are going to need to grow in order to accomplish what He has for you to achieve in the future.

As I look back on my life, I see how the things I was scared to try or the things that were my biggest uphill battles, were stepping stones for the next thing that God had for me.

Working through my fear of being vulnerable prepared me for a season of teaching women in which I share my personal struggles and growth. Getting over my idea that everything had to be perfect prepared me to work in a church setting where dealing with volunteer musicians sometimes left room for a "not so perfect" outcome. I needed to learn that it was not about a perfect performance, but about investing in the wonderful people with whom I was privileged to lead and help them grow in their gifts.

God is the perfect Father. And being a good Father to us means pushing us to the next challenge - He opens up doors for us. Maybe it's a new job; maybe it's a new opportunity; maybe it's a new relationship.

Sometimes He places us in situations that will require bravery; an obstacle that barges in on our comfortable lives; a conflict that takes prayerful wisdom and confron-tation; a situation that requires leadership or patience … each circumstance has the possibility to raise our level of courage.

Other times God will put a dream in your heart. Something that you just can't get away from. This very book is one of those things for me. An idea that began to grow in my heart that I just could not put aside. Of course, all my insecurities and inadequacies started shouting immediately in my head: "What if I fail?" "What if it's no good?" "What if no one wants to read it?" But more and more, God continually showed me that obedience was really the heart of the matter. In spite of all my questions and fears, the fact was that God had spoken to me and my job as His daughter is to always do what He says.

And the beautiful thing is, when God puts a dream in our heart and we take a step in obedience, God patiently leads us *all* the way. He's not like the dad at the pool who just throws his kid into the deep end and says, "You'll learn!" No! God patiently shows us how to stay afloat and leads us through our fear into courage.

I love the story of Gideon in Judges 6 - the Israelites had taken a serious beating by the Midianites, and they had all run and scattered into the mountains. The Midianites had then invaded their land and were stealing all the food, stripping all the land and destroying everyone and everything in their path.

That's where we find Gideon hiding. Hiding in a winepress crushing wheat; hiding from his enemies; hiding his food from the thieves. Suddenly, the angel of the Lord appeared to him and said, "Mighty hero, the Lord is with you!" (Judges 6:12) Then the Lord turned to him and said, "Go with the strength you have and rescue Israel from the Midianites. I am sending you." (Judges 6:14)

So was Gideon's response, "Absolutely Lord! I'm right on it ... boy have you picked the right guy?" No way. "But Lord," Gideon replied, "How can I rescue Israel? My clan is the weakest in the whole tribe of Manasseh, and I am the least in my entire family." Gideon was able to recite his every weakness, lack of qualification and shortcoming on the spot. God brought him a challenge and Gideon promptly replied, "This is too hard for me!" I don't think God was shocked by

Gideon's lack of confidence. So He replied to him, "I will be with you. And you will destroy the Midianites as if you were fighting against one man." (Judges 6:16)

God promised Gideon that He would go with him and that he would have victory over his enemies. Comforting words, right? But Gideon was still uncertain. So he asked God for a sign. Gideon replied, "If you are truly going to help me, show me a sign to prove that it is really the Lord speaking to me. (Judges 6:17) God's response to Gideon surprises me. He said, "Okay." Not, "How dare you question me! I have told you what to do, now get to work!" God gave Gideon the sign that he was looking for. Fire came down from heaven and consumed the sacrifice that Gideon had prepared, and this demonstration gave him the confidence to move forward and tear down the idols that God had told him to.

Then God gave him more direction. He was to lead the Israelite army into battle. So what does Gideon do? Again, he asks for a sign. He said, "If you are truly going to use me to rescue Israel as you promised, prove it to me in this way. I will put a wool fleece on the threshing floor tonight. If the fleece is wet with dew in the morning but the ground is dry, then I will know that you are going to help me rescue Israel as you promised." And that is just what happened: When Gideon got up early the next morning, he squeezed the fleece and wrung out a whole bowlful of water. (Judges 16:36-38)

So Gideon then got to work, right? Nope. He wanted another sign. Gideon said to God, "Please don't be angry with me, but let me make one more request. This time let the fleece remain dry while the ground around it is wet with dew." So that night God did as Gideon asked. The fleece was dry in the morning, but the ground was covered with dew. (Judges 6:39-40)

What I love about this story is that God allowed Gideon to ask for signs. He understood Gideon's insecurity and fear, and used these miracles to build his confidence that he was on the right path. I can relate. I often wonder, "God am I hearing you right? Am I really supposed to do what I think you're calling me to do?" I love the fact that God gives Gideon indicators along the way to say to him "You got it right! It's really me! Keep going!"

Each time God proved himself, Gideon's confidence grew a little more. Each time God showed up, Gideon felt He was with him. Each time God spoke, and Gideon heard Him correctly; he was more secure in his ability to hear clearly. With each sign, He proved to Gideon, "You and I are in this thing together and I'm able to do miracles beyond what your human mind can imagine."

I love that God patiently led Gideon through this new chapter of his life. I love that He was willing to hold his hand a little; I love that He reassured him. I think this was God's way of teaching Gideon to let go of his fear and face the new challenge that God had for him. He led him with patience and understanding.

And I believe God will lead you the same way. I think that He will give you signs to let you know you are on the right track. I think He will confirm and reconfirm His plan for you using His Word, through other godly counsel and with plain old miracles. When He puts a dream in your heart and a task in your hand, He will lead and guide you until its completion.

I think that nothing makes God prouder than when He sees you and I take up the challenge that He has before us and go for it. I think He loves to see us face our fears and do it anyway; I imagine his heart swells with pride when He watches His daughters step out into the unknown and take a chance. And I can almost hear His voice, cheering us on as we make our leap: "Come on baby - you can do it! Trust me! If you make the jump, I will *always* catch you."

CHAPTER 5

MY FATHER'S COMPANIONSHIP

There's a legendary story about my husband Jeff and his father John Kerr. Jeff grew up in Calgary, Alberta and enjoyed every minute of growing up surrounded by the mountains. His dad was a nature lover and was known to drag his kids off into some sort of outdoor adventure whenever the spirit moved him. There was never much planning or forethought put into these events, just a wing and a prayer.

One day he and Jeff decided to take a canoe up into the mountains at Lake Louise and go down the river to Banff. They drove up the mountain, put their canoe in the water, and began the daylong journey down the meandering river. As they reached the end of the trek and found themselves in Banff, it suddenly occurred to them that their car was back up in Lake Louise (two hours away) and they had no way to get back to it.

It began to rain, and they became soaked to the bone. So they began walking along the highway, with life vests still on and their canoe hidden in the woods. Eventually they hitch hiked their way back to their car and found their way back home, no worse for the wear.

Jeff loves to tell that story. He loves to talk about the day he was stranded with his dad. They love to reminisce about it and laugh at their self-induced circumstances and lack of organization. Jeff has hundreds of fond memories of moments spent in similar situations with his dad and he treasures each one of them.

Jeff carries on the tradition today with our children. He is fantastic about taking our kids out for one-on-one time with him. Snowy days spent on sledding hills; sunny days spent at a swimming pool; quiet days playing video games; crazy days spent on roller coasters. Each of our children are building up the same reservoir of memories of moments spent with their father and I'm so very thankful for it.

Generally, there has been a huge shift in the roles that fathers play in their children's lives in the last 50 years. It was quite typical for a man in the past to have limited involvement with the day-to-day lives of his children. His job was to bring home the money and discipline when needed. But many times there was a lack of companionship and friendship between fathers and children.

When Betty was about 18 months old, Jeff decided to take her up to Canada to visit his family. So, he booked a flight and made plans to spend a week at his brother's house – just him and Betts. I remember telling my 84-year-old grandmother about the trip. She could not believe that he was going to take care of that little girl all by himself. She kept saying, "And you're not going with him? Who is going to take care of the baby?" I would say, "Jeff is, Grandma!" and she would just shake her head. That would have been unheard of in her day.

The change of roles we have seen in parenting over the years has caused its share of problems, but it has also opened up the door for men to be fully entrenched in the lives of their kids. They are in the delivery room; they change diapers; they are at the school meetings; they share the daily responsibilities of raising their children. And so, I think it is becoming easier for us to envision a God that wants to be involved in every part of our lives.

One of the misconceptions that we discussed earlier was the view that God was distant and far off and uninterested in a personal relationship with us. Many of us see God as an authority and disciplinarian, but we cannot see Him as someone who is interested in being a part of our "everyday" lives.

But the truth is that God wants to enjoy an intensely personal, connected, companionship with you. He enjoys who you are; He wants to spend time with you; He wants to know what you are thinking and feeling; He wants to know everything about you and He wants you to know everything about Him.

When I was a freshman in Bible College, I remember walking down the hallway one day, and I saw a note on the door of the Dean of Women's office. She had written out Proverbs 3:32. It said, 'He is intimate with the upright." I remember stopping and staring at the word "intimate."

What a strange word that was for me to think of in regards to God.

He is *God*, the big huge God who created everything. How in the world could He be intimate with me? My heart skipped a beat at the idea that my relationship with God could be more than just service and duty, but that it could be deep and close and intimate.

Ironically, there was a time when we weren't allowed that "intimate access" to God the Father. In the Old Testament, the Temple was the place where the presence of God dwelled. As you entered the Temple, you walked into the outer courts. The women were only allowed to be in those external areas. Then came the inner courts where the altars for sacrifice were located. Then came the Holy Place and deep inside the center of the Temple was the Most Holy Place. This was the precise location where the presence of God dwelled. A huge curtain separated the Most Holy Place from the rest of the temple. No one was allowed to enter except for once a year when the High Priests were allowed to enter to offer a sacrifice for the people's sin.

We were separated from God. Because of our sinfulness and His holiness, there was no way we could just walk into the presence of God. We could not approach Him. This perfect God could not be in the same room with sinful people – so we were left out in the courtyard.

But something amazing happened when Jesus died on the cross. Mark 15:37&38 says, "Then Jesus uttered another loud cry and breathed His last. And then the curtain in the sanctuary of the Temple was torn in two, from top to bottom."

The veil was torn. The drape that kept us separate from God was removed. When Jesus died on the cross, He opened the door for us to have one-on-one access to God the Father. No longer did we need a priest or other third party to speak to Him on our behalf; no longer were we relegated to the outer courts; no longer were we separated from His presence. When that curtain was torn, Jesus provided a way for us to be close to the Father.

We can now talk to Him whenever we want. We can ask for anything, and know in confidence that He will hear our prayer. We can enter His presence and be close to His heart. You and I can enjoy Him and experience a close relationship to Him every single day.

Now, some of us may have never considered having that kind of relationship with God. Maybe in your mind, there is still a big veil separating you from Him. Maybe religion has taught you that you need someone else to speak to God for you. Maybe shame from your past has made you feel like you need that curtain to hide you and all the guilt you carry on the inside from the Father. Maybe you never imagined that you could be intimate with God – that you could talk to Him informally; you never realized that you could have a friendship with Him and enjoy His companionship in your life.

But the truth is that you *can* enjoy that kind of relationship with God. The truth is that He *desires* that kind of relationship with you. Psalm 25:14 in The Message says,

"God-friendship is for God-worshippers; they are the ones He confides in." Did you read that? It says that not only can you confide in God – but that He will confide in YOU! He will speak to you. He will unlock the secrets of His heart to you.

John 15:14 confirms this by saying, "You are my friends if you obey me. I no longer call you servants, because a master doesn't confide in his servants. Now you are my friends, since I have told you everything the Father has told me." We can enjoy a deeply personal relationship with God the Father.

Now, perhaps this idea of "friendship with the Father" feels very strange to you. Maybe you didn't enjoy a "companion" kind of relationship with your earthly father. Perhaps you've never had a person in authority be interested in you as a person. Maybe you've never experienced someone whom you admired and respected actually want to hear what you have to say and understand who you are as a person.

So what does an intimate, personal relationship with God look like? Many of us are used to compartmentalizing our faith. We view "God time" as the times when we are at church or reading the Bible or praying. But I truly believe that the kind of relationship He wants with us is one of constant companionship. Where we are aware of His presence with us throughout every day in every activity. Not relegated to the super spiritual, the crisis, or the extraordinary. He wants to be a part of the mundane, the pleasant, and the ordinary as well. He wants to be a part of ALL of it.

Why?

First of all, He likes to spend time with you. For so many of us, our idea of spending time with God has more to do with obligation than enjoyment. We know we're *supposed* to go to church; we're *supposed* to pray; we're *supposed* to read the Bible.

But what if the time we spent with God was out of the sheer enjoyment of being with Him. What if we laid all obligations aside, and instead sought to enjoy His company? I think it would revolutionize not only our church and devotional experiences, but our entire lives.

See, there are people who I like to be around. They are the people that encourage and uplift me; they are the people that make me laugh. When I spend time with them, I feel better about myself; I feel ready to tackle whatever comes my way; I dream bigger, dig deeper, and feel stronger. When I'm around someone who loves me, believes in me and supports me, I find myself believing the best about myself.

And, you will find no one better at bringing out the best in you than God the Father. When you invite Him along in your everyday life, His confidence, His purpose, and His unlimited resources will be revealed in your life. When you allow Him to show you His thoughts and intentions towards you, you start to believe it about yourself.

When you spend time with someone, you learn about them and they learn about you. You share your thoughts and feelings and ideas; you grow closer as you learn about each other.

Some of my most vivid memories of times with my Dad

are driving in the car. I remember talking about all kinds of things. School, friends, boys, politics, and Jesus. Those everyday conversations are the very things that shaped my ideas about life.

I remember one time as I was approaching the "dating age" where my dad and I were running an errand somewhere. He opened up the door for me and then walked around to the other side of the car. As he got in, he said, "Now, you make sure that boys open your car door for you. And when he's walking around, you reach over and unlock his door for him." (This was before power locks … I'm so old!) He continued on, "When a boy opens your door, it's a sign of respect, and when you unlock his, it's a way to say 'thank you' for respecting me." He also told me to take note of how a boy drove when we were out together. He said, "If a boy is driving recklessly, it's a bad sign. It shows a lack of concern for your safety and if he really cared about you, he would be more concerned about keeping you safe, than showing off."

I'm sure that my dad probably does not even remember that conversation with me. But to this day, I do not get in a car without checking to make sure that Jeff's door is unlocked. And I can't even count the times that I came home from a date determined to never go out with that boy again because of the way he drove.

Never underestimate the impact those simple, everyday moments can make in your relationship with God as well. I determined in my heart a few years ago to invite Jesus into my everyday life. When I changed my perspective from

having "God time" and then "regular time" and instead
determined to live every day "with" God, I have seen growth
I never thought was possible.

And although He still speaks to me when I am doing
my devotions, praying, or in church, it's in those everyday
moments that I find God speaking most clearly. Most of my
great times with God are when I am cleaning my house or
doing the dishes and I am just thinking about God. Other
times it's when I'm driving in my car and I just start talking
to Him. An then there are the times when I don't know how
to discipline a child, or which decision to make, or what to
say to a friend in need. I invite him into every situation,
whether great or small, and He becomes my advisor, coun-
selor and confidant.

Every relationship grows when you spend time together.
And your relationship with God is no different. The more
you acknowledge His presence in your life every single day,
the more you'll see your trust in Him grow; you'll see your
reliance on Him deepen; and mostly, you'll understand the
depths of His love for you more and more.

So, how do we develop that everyday relationship with
God? Just start talking to Him! You don't need fancy words
or a specific structure to your prayers. Just start talking to
Him the way you would talk to one of your best friends.
Tell Him what you're worried about; tell Him what you're
confused about; tell Him what your excited about - He
wants all of it!

I think many times we feel like we need to edit ourselves
with God. We don't think we can tell Him the things we're

struggling with. We think we need to present ourselves to Him in "perfect" form; we think that if we question how He is working, it is somehow a lack of faith. But I have come to realize that absolute honesty is vital for my relationship with God. It's pointless for me to only offer the positive parts of my life and leave out the questions and struggles. The truth is that God is big enough to handle your questions. He is not shocked and horrified by your mistakes - He wants us to bring those things to Him so that he can help us work through those failures and struggles.

Another way to develop your relationship with the Father is by reading the Bible. The Bible is God's love letter to you. It is full of compliments, advice and more than anything, it gives us a beautiful picture of who God our Father really is. There is no better place to learn about Him, His character and the type of relationship He desires to have with you.

Hebrews 4:12 says, "For the word of God is full of living power. It is sharper than the sharpest knife, cutting deep into our innermost thoughts and desires." The words written in the scriptures have supernatural power. They are able to speak directly into the parts of us that are in need.

I can't tell you the number of times I have found direction or comfort or reassurance when I have opened up the Bible searching for truth. So often the exact answer I am looking for or the encouragement I need I find in the Word.

God wants to meet with you; He wants to connect with you through his Word; He wants to encourage you through His Spirit; He wants to talk to you and speak to your heart every moment of every day. For you see my friends, the reality is this: God really likes to spend time with you – because He really *likes* you; He loves your personality; He *enjoys* you.

One of the things that I was most surprised about when I became a mother was how much I *liked* my children. I always knew that I would love them. But I was unprepared for how much I really enjoyed who they are as people. I really like to talk to them. I think they have really great personalities. Their quirky traits and funny comments make me laugh and I like hanging out with them.

It might surprise you to realize that God really likes you. He loves you beyond anything you could comprehend, but He's also really fond of you; He smiles at your wit; He is impressed with your intellect; He thinks you are a pretty cool chick.

I love this verse in Zechariah 2:8 (NIV), "For this is what the LORD Almighty says: "After He has honored me and has sent me against the nations that have plundered you—for whoever touches you touches the apple of His eye."

You are the apple of His eye. You are someone who He desires to spend time with; He is crazy about you; He desires that your relationship to be a deep, meaningful and comfortable companionship with Him.

CHAPTER 6

The Discipline of the Father

I'm always amazed at how different each one of my children is. There is Lucy, who is sweet and thoughtful. There's Charlie, who's smart and introspective. There's Betty, who is sassy and compassionate. And baby Dorothy, who seems to be blessed with both a sweet disposition AND a bit of a temper. I am intrigued by the fact that each one of them approaches life so differently; how they learn; how they relate to other people; and especially, how they respond to discipline.

I have to constantly re-think how I'm going to handle a situation based on which kid I am dealing with. Lucy is eager to please, and will usually comply with a little pressure. Charlie usually gets in trouble because he has forgotten what the rules are. Nevertheless, he is quick to repent – big tears and heartfelt "sorrys." Then there's Betty. She doesn't mind testing the limits a bit. And it takes a lot more effort and a lot more consistency for her to learn her lesson.

Jeff recently stumbled upon her outside breaking all the

sidewalk chalk into tiny little pieces. He told her to stop, and of course, she asked "Why?". Jeff said, "Because it isn't nice to break toys. How would you like it if I broke one of your toys?" She gave a little smirk and said, "Okay, let's do it!" So Jeff got a little more specific. "Okay Betty, how would you like it if I broke your Dora doll?" The quick-witted three year old replied once again, "OKAY!" So Jeff said, "I think you would be really sad if I cut off the head of your favorite doll." He watched as she processed what her dad was suggesting and suddenly a huge smile came across her face and she said, "I'll go get her!" She then ran into the house and pulled a pair of scissors out of the drawer. Yep, that kid is a little more challenging to discipline!

Unlike my three year old, when I was a kid, I hated getting in trouble. Hated it. Every year, my New Year's resolution was to not get in trouble at all. (I didn't say I was a realistic child...) I never got in trouble at school. I never broke the rules. (Well, almost never.)

What is it about being disciplined that bothers me so much? I think I genuinely feel bad that I behaved poorly. I think it's embarrassing to be caught in the wrong. It's a blow to the ego. I hate feeling like I've let down my parents or anyone else, for that matter. The thought of consequences is no picnic either. No one wants to endure the repercussions of discipline.

So, how do you respond to discipline? Are you, like me, terrified of getting in trouble? Do you like to push the limits as far as you can? When you find yourself in the midst of discipline, is your first response to fight back? Are you a quick learner, or does it take you a lot of time and tears before you learn your lesson?

However you tend to respond to earthly discipline, chances are you have a similar response when God is disciplining you. Because of my fear of discipline, when I would stumble upon passages in the Bible concerning this topic, I would quickly pass over them and move on to a different subject. I just didn't want to think about God in that way.

I have come to realize that this is, by far, one of the greatest roadblocks between me and God the Father. This is where the part of me that is scared of God comes into play. I'm afraid of His discipline. I'm worried that He is angry with me. I am fearful of letting Him down and feeling like He isn't going to love me any more if I make a mistake.

So, I am really trying to gain a better understanding of God's discipline. Why does He correct us? What is the motivation behind His instruction? What does His discipline look like? And what doesn't it look like?

We all know that good parents discipline their children. These little people come to us as blank slate, and we are to shape them. We set up boundaries and then we are responsible to hold them accountable for staying within those boundaries. It's how they learn what is right and wrong. It's how they learn what is ok and what is not ok.

It's how we prepare them to make the right choices in their life. How they should treat other people. What their legacy will be. Their good name, their reputation; the mark that they will make on the world.

It's also how we keep them safe. We say, "Don't touch!"

and "Don't go there!" It's how we teach them to be productive and responsible. We make sure they are home on time so they'll be a punctual adult. We teach them not to break toys, so they learn the value of their possessions.

Proverbs 13:24 says, "Those who spare the rod of discipline hate their children. Those who love their children care enough to discipline them." I want the best for my kids, and so I care enough about them to make sure they are well-behaved little people who will grow up into well-behaved big people.

It certainly isn't easy though. I remember one of the first times I disciplined Lucy. She was fairly young, and had started throwing a temper tantrum. I had warned her that if she didn't stop, she wasn't going to be able to go to the Science Museum with a special friend the next day. I kept threatening and threatening, and she just wouldn't stop. So, I finally had to follow through. (Yes, this was my first time … now days there would be a lot less threatening and a lot more action.)

I remember making the phone call to our friends saying that Lucy would not be going on the trip. I could hear her up in her room sobbing at the disappointment. I felt so bad; I sat down at the kitchen table, laid my head down and started sobbing myself. I hated punishing her, but I knew that I had to follow through or else she would never learn.

And just as we discipline our children because we love them and want them to be better, God disciplines us. We are His children. Galatians 4:6-7 says, "And because you Gentiles have become His children, God has sent the Spirit of His son into your hearts, and now you can call God you dear Father. Now you are no longer a slave, but God's own child. And since you are His child, everything He has belongs to you."

God is our Father. It is His job to point us on the right path. He needs to show us where we are making bad decisions. He needs to reveal to us where our priorities are out of balance. He needs to show us where we are not growing, or where our behaviors or attitudes are not what they should be.

He sets the boundaries and then holds us accountable for staying within them. Hebrews 12:5-6 in The Message says, "Or have you forgotten how good parents treat children and that God regards you as His children? My dear child, don't shrug off God's discipline, but don't be crushed by it either. It's the child He loves that He disciplines; the child He embraces, He also corrects."

This is one specific area in our lives where our experiences with our earthly fathers (or mothers, or anyone else in authority) can make a big difference in how we react to God's discipline. In order to understand your reactions to God's correction, it's important to look at how you were disciplined as a child and your reaction to it.

Perhaps discipline in your home was arbitrary. You may have never known how or when the hammer was going to drop. Sometimes the rules were enforced, and other times you were able to get away with anything. Or perhaps one time the punishment was reasonable, given calmly and

I am inconsistent in parenting

lovingly, and then the next time it was a harsh reaction doled out in anger and frustration.

This kind of hit or miss discipline could cause you to feel insecure about your relationships. You never really know what to expect – and so there is a level of uncertainty. Perhaps you feel insecure about God's discipline. You might think to yourself, 'God may be gracious to me this time, but next time, He's going to let me have it!"

Maybe discipline in your home was based on fear and blame. You might have been afraid of being punished or scared of doing something wrong. You might have thought, "I better not make a mistake, or else…." And because of this, you have a hard time feeling relaxed and safe with God. You are always wondering if He is mad at you. You shield yourself from feeling vulnerable with God out of self protection. You are always wondering when He is going to let you have it.

Was there a lack of discipline in your home? The absence of boundaries can cause us to feel unloved and not cared for. It's as if no one cares enough about you to stop you from behaving poorly. If this was your experience, you may view God as uninterested in you. Or you may not have respect for His authority in your life. You might have a hard time believing that He will hold you accountable for your sin and discipline you in love.

And the greatest reality of all is that even in healthy discipline, we all had childish responses to our parents. We didn't see the love and concern to learn a better way. Oh no! We said, "You're so unfair!" We thought, "You just don't want me to have any fun!" Or perhaps we just came to the conclusion that "You're just mean."

The truth of the matter is that we all have "baggage" regarding discipline that can affect our relationship with God the Father. Whatever kind of earthly discipline you have received, the most important thing for you to comprehend is that GOD is a PERFECT Father. He doesn't ever make mistakes. He is all knowing and He always disciplines us appropriately. There is no way that God can ever treat you imperfectly. It's absolutely not possible.

Hebrews 12:7 says, "But God's discipline is always right and good for us because it means we will share in His holiness. No discipline is enjoyable while it's happening – it is painful. But afterward there will be a quiet harvest of right living for those who are trained in this way." God's discipline is always right. It is always exactly what we need at exactly the right time. He knows every thought you have, every preparation you need, and every weakness that needs transformation. And He knows exactly how to weed it out of your life - God's discipline is perfect.

I'm so thankful for that. Now that I am a parent, I recognize how, at times, I lash out at my kids in anger. Or I let them get away with something that I really should have stepped up and corrected. As a human, I know that there are times when I fail to discipline correctly. But how wonderful, I can know that God's discipline is always going to be executed in love and perfection.

Understanding the truth of God's discipline can be hard to grasp. I can have a hard time wrapping my head around the fact that He *always* knows exactly how to handle me and my weaknesses. It is so easy for me to put those human shortcomings on God. I am realizing that there is a fundamental flaw in my understanding of what God's discipline really is; I think that I many times, I confuse discipline with punishment.

I have a friend whose mother is a "punisher." I think she feels it is her job to punish the people around her who don't live up to her expectations. If you say something she doesn't like, you get the silent treatment. If you choose not to take her advice, you will be "uninvited" to family functions for a while. If you behave inappropriately, you have to endure her wrath for an extended amount of time. No one knows how long she'll stay mad, just an arbitrary amount of time to be determined by her. Long enough until she's made her point. Long enough until you feel bad enough to satisfy her. Long enough until she feels like you have paid appropriately for your wrongs.

I have watched her children sink in frustration …"Mom's mad again." I have sensed their insecurity when they are never sure how long they are going to have to pay for their missteps. I have seen the hurt in their eyes when they feel, once again, that they have let her down.

I think many of us view God as a "punisher." We think that when we have screwed up, He just gets mad at us. We think He will withhold His love just to make us pay for our failures.

 But there is a big difference between punishment and discipline; there is a huge difference between consequences and retaliation. The chasm between grace and judgment is immeasurable.

God disciplines us. If you look at the root of the word – it is *disciple*. To disciple someone is to take them under your wing and show you how to do it better. When God disciplines us, it is not punishment. Actually, punishment by definition is "a penalty that is imposed on someone for wrong." Yes, our behaviors break God's laws. Yes, there is a penalty for our sin. But the beautiful thing is that God pays the penalty for us! Romans says, 'Yet, God, with unde-served kindness, declares that we are righteous. He did this through Christ Jesus when He freed us from the penalty for our sins. (Romans 3:8) Punishment is not needed when we look to Jesus. If we ask Jesus to forgive us for our shortcom-ings – the penalty is paid in full. No need to drag it out. It's a done deal.

The definition for punishment is "rough treatment." Harsh. Ungracious. Designed with the intent to hurt – not the intent to restore. Some of us have the view that God is so disappointed in us … that He just wants to make us pay.

But nothing could be further from the truth. God's disci-pline is always done in love. He desires for us to grow. He wants to help us work through the things that could hurt us or cause us to not reach our full potential. So when He disciplines us, it is motivated by His desire to see us *do* or *be* better.

I John 4:16 says, "God is love … there is no fear in love. But perfect love drives out fear, because fear has to do with punishment. The one who fears is not made perfect in love." If you fear the discipline of God, it reveals a lack of understanding of the loving nature of God. When we are confident in God's love for us, we aren't afraid of His hand.

There is no reason for us to fear God's correction. Job 5:17-18 says, "But consider the joy of those corrected by God. Do not despise the chastening of the Almighty when you sin. For though He wounds, He also bandages. He strikes, but His hands also heal."

We can trust His discipline. He always meets us right where we are at and shows us the perfect way to learn our lesson. I don't discipline my three year old because she didn't do the laundry. I don't ground my eight year old from using the car. A good parent finds correction that teaches. We provide punishment that is suitable for the maturity and disposition of the child. And God the Father is no different. He leads you along your walk of faith and guides you appropriately and graciously.

Sometimes I feel like God must be so sick of teaching me how to do it better. I feel like I should already know – and not have to be told. But I think God the Father understands His role in our life and expects to discipline us in love. In Psalms it says, "The Lord is like a father to His children, tender and compassionate to those who fear Him. For He understands how weak we are; He knows we are only dust." (Psalm 103:13-14)

As a parent, I understand that part of my job is to discipline my children. It just comes with the territory. I expect it. I understand that it is necessary. I don't react in personal disappointment when my kids need correction. That's what I'm there for! If they did it right the first time around, they wouldn't need me at all.

And the same is true with our heavenly Father. He wants to be there to point out our shortcomings (because we will always have them, won't we!) and be there to lovingly, with tenderness and compassion; show us a better way. It's His job.

Knowing we can trust God's discipline should radically change our perspective. Not only should we not fear the hand of our Father, we should embrace His discipline. This is a sign of maturity and growth in our lives, when we can appreciate the correction we are given.

I remember one time when I was in junior high, when I got in trouble. I was in our church youth choir, and we would rehearse on Wednesday night after youth group. The director had a rule that if you were more than five minutes late for rehearsal, then you couldn't stay for practice that week. One week, my friends and I were goofing around after church, and didn't realize what time it was. When we showed up ten minutes late, the director told us that we had to leave. When my dad picked me up, I began to tell him about her silly rules and how she was soooo unreasonable to expect us to not be late. (Insert snotty-fourteen-year-old-girl-attitude here…)

My father calmly informed me that the next day he was going to drive me to the director's office at church and I was to apologize for being late and getting kicked out of choir. Needless to say, I was mortified. I remember crying all day at school in anticipation for my afternoon meeting. And sure enough, my dad picked me up from school (having taken off work himself) and drove me to the church and sat me down to meet with her. I apologized (in between sobs) for being late and promised never to do it again.

That was a really huge moment for me. While I was going through it, I was absolutely devestated. I thought my dad was totally overreacting and making a big deal out of nothing. But now when I look back, I have a completely different perspective. I think my dad saw my little four-teen-year-old attitude that wasn't entirely respectful of my teacher and the rules that she set up. I think he took that opportunity to put a marker in the ground that said, "You are going to respect those in authority over you" and "You are going to follow the rules no matter how silly you think they might be." Now, I am so thankful that my dad set a standard that high for me to follow; I'm glad that he made it very clear what kind of attitude I was expected to have. I have a very different perspective now.

As we grow in our faith in Christ, we should begin to appreciate the process that is weeding out those things in our hearts that keep us from reaching our full potential in Christ. Psalm 119:75 says, "I know, O Lord, that your decisions are fair; you disciplined me because I needed it." A mature view of God's correction can admit that we have areas in our lives that need to be transformed. We can admit that we need it!

Embracing God's discipline involves letting go of our immature ideas about punishment. We need to ask God to heal the wounds left by unfair or unloving discipline in our past. We need to recognize the truth of God's loving correction and let go of the pictures of Him that are inaccurate.

When you find yourself facing discipline, you need to ask yourself, "What are you trying to teach me?" "What is going on in my heart or behavior that has brought me here?" "What should I take away from this, and how can I grow more mature and strong in my walk with Christ through this lesson?" Psalm 119:71 says, "The suffering you sent was good for me, for it taught me to pay attention to your principles."

Discipline brings about growth. We all should desire growth. Transformation is a key component in our walk with Jesus. If we are in a relationship with him, we should constantly have things being weeded out of our life. New lessons should be learned. Old habits should be falling by the wayside. Growth is the mark of maturity.

We've got to get past our pride that doesn't like to have our wrongs pointed out. We've got to let go of our ego that thinks we can do no wrong. We've got to seek those things that will shape and mold us into the image of Christ.

I think Hebrews 12:7-11 in The Message sums it up beautifully. It says, "God is educating you; that's why you must never drop out. He's treating you as dear children. This trouble you're in isn't punishment; it's training, the normal experience of children. Only irresponsible parents leave children to fend for themselves. Would you prefer an irresponsible God? We respect our own parents for training and not spoiling us, so why not embrace God's training so we can truly live? While we were children, our parents did what seemed best to them. But God is doing what is best for us, training us to live God's holy best. At the time, discipline isn't much fun. It always feels like it's going against the grain. Later, of course, it pays off handsomely, for it's the well-trained who find themselves mature in their relationship with God. "

CHAPTER 7

THE COMFORT OF MY FATHER'S ARMS

A few years ago I was at a conference for pastors. I was sitting in a session where the speaker was talking about burnout and dealing with difficult times in your ministry. He began to share a very personal story about his family and the struggles they had gone through a few years earlier.

He found himself facing a growing number of obstacles in his life, and the trials were starting to pile one on top of another until he felt like he couldn't see the light of day anymore. At the center of this struggle, was his teenage daughter.

A season of rebellion had spiraled downward into a pattern of self destruction and depression that left this sweet girl lost to her family and those closest to her. She was wasting away from a severe eating disorder; she was sneaking out of the house, doing drugs, and getting into all kinds of trouble. All attempts her parents made to reach out to her were rebuffed in anger and resentment.

One night, they received a phone call saying that their

daughter had been arrested for shoplifting. As they brought her home in silence, this father found himself desperately crying out to God for some sort of breakthrough.

When they arrived home, she immediately went up to her room and shut the door. The father felt impressed by the Holy Spirit to go up to talk to her - he gently knocked, only to receive harsh words and a demand to leave her alone,

but he pressed on. He slowly opened up the door and found his beautiful little girl curled up on her bed – just staring ahead. The father walked over to where she was, laid down next to her and wrapped his big arms around her. Initially, she stiffened and tried to move away, but he was determined not to let go. Then, in an instant, he felt her body relax and suddenly a wave of tears opened into a flood of emotion. As she sobbed through her pain and regret, the father held her tighter and tighter and whispered, "it's okay … I love you … it's okay … you're going to be alright … we're going to make it."

As I listened to his story, tears streamed down my face and I felt God speak to my heart. He said, "This is what I want to do with my daughters. So many of them are hurting, lost, and feeling bad about themselves. They feel alone and don't think that anyone sees or hears them. But I want to wrap my arms around them and show them how much I love them; the comfort they will find in my arms will forever change their lives."

Jesus echoes the Father's heart in Matthew when He looks out over the city of Jerusalem and His heart breaks for the people of the city who are lost, alone, and hurting. "How often I've ached to embrace your children, the way a hen gathers her chicks under her wings, and you wouldn't let me." (Matthew 23:7 MSG) God longs to wrap you in His arms and whisper words of reassurance and love.

Comfort, by definition, is to cause relief from a stressful situation. To comfort someone is to console them, to soothe or cheer them. It is to relieve the anxiety, and replace it with calm reassurance.

We all have felt the comfort of someone caring for us in a moment of need. Perhaps it was a kind word during the loss of a loved one; maybe it was a tender embrace when faced with heartache or need; or maybe it was just a steady presence that reassured us that we were not alone.

I hate it when my kids get hurt. I hate it when I see that look of confusion and pain in their eyes. But I love that when they skin their knee, I'm the first one they look for. They come running to me with big tears in their eyes and unwavering faith that I will somehow be able to make it all better.

I truly believe with all my heart, that God the Father feels exactly the same way about His children. He LOVES to comfort us in our time of need. He loves to hold us close and reassure us; He loves to speak words of comfort to us that calm our fears and quiet our anxieties; He wants us to come running to Him with our hurts in unwavering faith that He will somehow be able to make it all better.

Isaiah 40:1-2 says, "Comfort, comfort my people," says your God. "Speak tenderly to Jerusalem. Tell her that her sad days are gone and her sins are pardoned." God desires to speak the words into your heart that will bring peace to your soul and assure you that He is with you.

Why is the knowledge that God wants to be our comforter so important? Because we live in a world that takes its toll on us, don't we? It's easy to feel overwhelmed and weighed down by our obligations and roles. It's easy to feel isolated and lonely and think that no one sees us or is interested in what's going on inside of us.

And in this life, we get hurt; other people hurt us; circumstances come in and smash our hopes and dreams - life has a way of throwing us around and many of us are walking around broken and battered.

I know that as a woman, I often don't take the time to address the things that are going on in my heart. The pace of my life, the number of obligations, and the needs of everyone around me seem to take precedence. I find myself pushing down the aches in my heart and not addressing those places in need of comfort and reassurance.

And sometimes I don't think anyone else is aware of what's going on inside of me. I don't want to bother anyone else with my "stuff" or I don't know if anyone will understand. Or even more, I don't know how to articulate what I am feeling and needing. I don't realize that I am empty - that I'm disappointed - that I feel invisible or lost.

Who can I go to with all of these things? Although my husband loves me deeply, my girlfriends are always there to listen and my family is supportive, there is nowhere else that I can bring my deepest longing and need but the arms of my Heavenly Father. No one else knows my heart like He does;

no one knows just what to say to comfort my spirit. Psalm 42:7-8 says, "Deep calls to deep in the roar of your waterfalls; all your waves and breakers have swept over me. By day the Lord directs His love, at night His song is with me – a prayer to the God of my life." (NIV) The deep places of me can only be touched by the deep places of Him ... nothing else can even come close.

So, how does our Heavenly Father comfort us? First of all, He listens to us; He is engaged in our struggle; He's just there.

How many times have you said these words to someone you love, "I don't want you to fix it, I just want you to listen."? A lot of times, I am not looking for someone to find a solution to my problem, I just want to be heard. I want to know that I'm not alone and that someone is walking with me through my struggle.

The word "comfort" to me does not imply fixing. It is not focused on removing the obstacle or finding a solution. That may come later, but in the moment, comfort implies a presence within the pain.

One of the most intimate moments I have experienced with my husband was during the birth of our son. I went into pre-term labor, and was sent in an ambulance to a hospital with a neonatal intensive care unit. Jeff followed behind the ambulance in our car, but my labor was progressing rapidly. By the time we reached the hospital, the baby was in distress and they were running my gurney down the corridor for an emergency C-section.

I don't ever recall being as terrified as I was in that moment.

Everyone was rushing around me, speaking in terms that I didn't understand, and I was completely by myself. They took me into the operating room and were prepping me for the surgery when all of the sudden, in walked my husband in hospital scrubs. He sat down next to me and our eyes locked. We were both terrified and our eyes were brimming with tears. He took my hand and gave me this look – a look that was filled with both compassion and strength. It was a look that was full of love and assurance. I will never forget the comfort I found in that moment. Without a single word, Jeff's presence reassured me and I felt the fear begin to dissipate.

My friend, no matter what you are facing, God is with you. He is there. You might feel alone, but you are most certainly *not* alone. His presence can speak unspeakable comfort to you in your moment of greatest need. Without a word, He can quiet your spirit with the knowledge that He is there.

Another way that God brings comfort to us, is by bringing healing to the very wounds that are causing our pain. When my kids come running with a scrape on their knee, I hold them close and wipe their tears, and then I get to work. I gently wash out the cut, put some kind of ointment on it and then cover it with a band-aid and a kiss.

The Bible talks many times about God doing the same thing to us. Psalm 147:3 says, "He heals the brokenhearted, binding up their wounds." God not only wants to wipe away your tears, He wants to tend to the hurts that are causing the tears in the first place.

Maybe this whole book has opened your eyes to some wounds that you've been carrying around in your heart. You find yourself conflicted about the idea of God as your Father, because you still have so many hurts in relation to your earthly father. I believe with all my heart, that God wants to take that pain, and cover it with His love, and bring complete and total healing to your heart.

Maybe it's another person that has wounded your heart, a husband, a boyfriend, friend, or a pastor ... God does not want you to carry those cuts and bruises around anymore. He desires for you to walk in freedom and healing, not constantly reliving the pain of the past. Only through His supernatural power, can you truly be healed. Psalm 68:5-6 says, "Father to the fatherless, defender of widows- this is God, whose dwelling is holy. God places the lonely in families; He sets the prisoners free and gives them joy."

When we invite Him into those deep places of hurt, His loving hands mend and heal, bind and soothe, restore and redeem. He gently tends to those places and we find ourselves free from the baggage of the past and living our lives in the fullness He intended for us.

Our Father loves to comfort us. It brings Him great joy when He gets to hold you close and whisper words of comfort in your ear. He always wants to be the one to whom we run with our pain.

Deuteronomy 33:27 says, "The eternal God is your refuge, and His everlasting arms are under you." In my moment of greatest need - in those times when I wonder if anyone hears - if anyone knows, if anyone cares, I find great comfort in the thought of my Father's *everlasting arms* holding me. And if I listen closely, I can hear His whisper, "It's okay … I love you … it's okay … you're going to be alright … we're going to make it."

CHAPTER 8

My Protective Father

My extended family takes a vacation together every year. We go up to Northern Minnesota with my sister, her husband and kids, as well as my parents and grandparents. The first year that Jeff and I were married, we were all there and decided to go for a hike. As we walked through the woods, we came upon a crevice that looked down onto a lovely little stream. It was so beautiful, so I went walking over to the edge to get a closer look. Suddenly I heard a loud, panicked voice from behind me: "Kristine Elizabeth Lane! Get away from there! You are too close to the edge – you are going to fall!!!!" I was startled by the severity of the warning; I turned to see my dad with an intense look in his eyes, sternly shaking his finger at me.

Much to his dismay, I started to giggle - as did my husband (and everyone else). "Dad, not only am I no where near the edge, I'm 25 years old ... chill out!" We all had a good laugh at my poor dad's over-reaction. "Sorry," he said, "old habits die hard."

You can't really blame the guy. He had spent the last 25 years watching over me and making sure I was okay.

Coming to my aid when a teacher was being unfair; scoping out each new venture to make sure it was safe; lecturing every boy who wanted to take me out on a date about not driving too fast or staying out too late.

My husband really is looking forward to the days when our girls start dating. Something in him can't wait to scare those poor boys to death before they take his daughters out. He once heard a quote from the actor, Bruce Willis about raising daughters that he can't wait to use someday. Mr. Willis said, "I tell every boy that comes to date my daughter, 'Whatever you do to her, I'm going to do to you.'"

There is something in a father that is protective of his daughters. And there's something very comforting about knowing your father is watching over you. There's a security that awakens in you when you realize that someone has your back and is making sure that you are safe.

Especially as women, one of our greatest needs is the desire for security. To provide security for someone is to protect them; it is to watch over them and guard them; it is to take care of someone.

My husband (in contrast to my father) is a bit of an "under-reactor." He tends not to get too worked up about stuff, and doesn't have a penchant for worry. Shortly after we were married, Minneapolis was hit with a huge snow-storm. My sister and I were shopping and suddenly her cell phone rang. Her husband, Rick (again, more of the "over-reacting" type), was on the line. "Where are you?" he said with a panic. "The storm is too bad for you to drive. Stay put and I'll come pick you up." So, I thought, I had better call Jeff because I'm *sure* he's worried about me too. So I called him and said, "I hear the roads are getting bad, what should I do?" His response was, "Just drive home. If you go in a ditch, we can always pull you out." I was less than thrilled with his concern for me. When I got home I tried to explain to him how important it is for a woman to feel like someone is looking out for her. I told him, "I just want to feel like you are protecting me."

To his credit, this is something that has really grown in Jeff throughout our marriage. I have had four very difficult pregnancies and I can't remember ever feeling as secure and loved as when he's shooing me off to rest or holding my hand while we wait for a doctor, or constantly asking how I'm feeling; I love feeling like he's watching out for me.

And then there are his kids - heaven forbid anyone ever mess with one of them. The very thought of it makes his lips purse together and his face turn red. And it's very different than my "momma bear" protectiveness. It's less of an emotional reaction as it is a deep-seeded sense of responsibility. Perhaps it's territorial; perhaps it's testosterone. Whatever it is, there's no doubt in my mind that he would take on an army in order to protect me and his children from anyone or anything.

Many of you have never felt that feeling of being protected. Perhaps you never had a father in your life that was checking things out for you, or fighting for you, or keeping trouble at bay. Worse than that, for some of you your father was the source of harm. Instead of being the hand that shielded you from danger, he was the hand that caused you pain.

What is it about feeling protected that touches the core of us as women? Why is that so important to us? No matter how independent I am, there is still something in me that needs to feel looked after.

I was looking around online, and I came across a chat room where women were discussing this question: Do women really want to be protected? The answers were very intriguing. One woman stated that if her man was fighting for her, it would show his devotion to her and demonstrate that he really cares. Another lady shared that she likes the feeling of being around someone who is strong and capable and in control – that it made her feel more secure. I could relate to all the things these women were saying - feeling protected is very important to a woman's heart.

I realize one of the greatest struggles in my life is fear and anxiety. I am fearful something will happen to my husband or my children. I am fearful we won't have enough money. I am fearful because we live in a world where there are so many things to be fearful of!!

And I know I'm not the only one! Some of you are afraid of being alone; some of you are terrified your husband is going to walk out on you; some of you are won't go to a certain part of town or get on an airplane; some of you worry about getting sick; some of you are scared about your financial future.

Fear can be a debilitating thing. Our hearts start racing and our minds begin imagining all kinds of scenarios. We become overwhelmed with a feeling of helplessness. We think "There's nothing I can do to stop this." We feel lost and out of control. And once we embrace our fears, they can grow and grow. One area of worry can lead to another area of worry and pretty soon we find ourselves consumed with anxiety.

Because there is so much to be afraid of; because fear can grab a hold of us in so many areas; because, in my heart I *long* for someone to make me feel safe and secure, there are fewer attributes about My Heavenly Father I love more than this: God is my *protector*.

He says that He will hold me in His hand and keep me safe. He watches over me night and day and never closes His eyes to rest. He calls himself a fortress, a strong tower, a refuge and a shield - God is our protector.

As loved as I feel when Jeff is watching out for me, it is nothing compared to the security I should have in knowing that God is always watching over me. Psalm 91:1-2 says, "Those who live in the shelter of the Most High will find rest in the shadow of the Almighty. This I declare about the Lord: He alone is my refuge, my place of safety; He is my God, and I trust Him."

I admit that sometimes I can be confused about this attribute of God. If He is my protector, wouldn't it mean that nothing bad would ever happen? That any time evil was coming near me, God would intervene and stop it?

As I have sought to understand this (and I still have my questions that will have to wait for heaven....) God has shown me that He protects us in two different ways: Sometimes He protects us *from* trouble, and other times He protects us *in* trouble.

There are times when God, according to His will and His plan, will stop something from happening in order to protect us. Psalm 114 says, "He stands before me as a shield." What was coming my way to harm me could not touch me because God stood before me as a fortress.

My friend Jennifer experienced God's protection a few years ago during a horrible accident. Here is her story in her own words.

It happened in March of 2005. Rosie and Riley had just had their third birthday the week before. It was the first really nice spring day, and I had opened up all of the windows to air out the house. I was making dinner, and watching the kids run in and out playing a game where they would talk back and forth to each other from the deck to Ryan's bedroom window.

Apparently at some point they went into the twins' room, and climbed up on the dresser in front of the window (something Rosie had never done before - Riley was always the naughty climber!). Rosie stepped up onto the windowsill, leaned into the screen and went right through. Ryan came running into the kitchen jumping up and down, laughing nervously and yelling "Rosie fell out of the window!" over and over. Everything seriously went into that bizarre slow motion like you see in the movies. I ran down the hallway and looked into their room to see an empty window with no screen … and no Rosie. However, I could hear her screaming - which was the best sound in the world!

I ran back to the kitchen, picked up the phone and dialed 911, and then handed the phone to Ryan (who had just turned six), then I ran outside and down the deck stairs. She had fallen out face first, fell 15 feet, and landed flat on her stomach on still-frozen ground. By the time I got there, she was just starting to try to get herself up, so I just cradled the back of her head and neck in my arms and rolled her over flat onto her back. I was honestly, completely convinced she had to have broken her back ... and who knows what else.

It seriously felt like 30 minutes went by before anyone arrived, but it was only a couple of minutes. Police were first on scene, then one fire truck, another fire truck and another police car. It was very frustrating because there were at least 15 men standing around us in a half circle, but nobody was DOING anything, no one would even touch her - they were waiting for the para-medics to arrive.

Finally the ambulance showed up, and the medics put a c-collar on her and moved her to a spinal board. When they carried her around to the front of the house, I realized that the entire neighborhood was watching. I asked if we could go to Children's Hospital, but the medics told me they had to take her to Regions because it was a Level 1 Trauma Center. So much for reassurance!

The transport took almost 40 minutes - longest drive of my life. Rosie screamed at the top of her lungs the ENTIRE time. I don't have any recollection of anything the medic did for her other than putting on an oxygen mask. I tried to get her to sing the ABCs with me, told her funny stories, but she just kept crying.

When we arrived at Regions, there was a crowd of doctors and nurses standing in the door waiting for us. They whisked Rosie away and took me to a separate room to do all the paperwork - I could hear her screaming the whole time. At some point, she finally quieted down, and I wasn't sure if that was a good thing or not! After what felt like an eternity, a nurse finally came and got me and took me to the ER. A female doctor came out and said "Well, mom ... I cannot find ANYTHING wrong with her. NOTHING. She is totally fine." She took me into the room and there was Rosie, sitting on the bed in her tiny little gown, all smiles and eating a popsicle. Not a single broken bone; no internal injuries - nothing. Just a tiny pink spot on her forehead from where her head had hit the ground (and that was gone within about two hours). I just about collapsed on the floor right then and there.

To this day, I still get choked up thinking about it - what an incredibly close call it was. I honestly believe that Rosie's angels just floated her down and landed her safely on the ground. God most definitely had His hand of protection on her that day.

Sweet little Rosie is a living example of Psalm 91:11-12, which says, "He ordered His angels to guard you wherever you go. If you stumble, they'll catch you." (MSG) God was a shield of protection for her.

There are times when God sees something that could harm you or I, and He keeps it at bay and will not allow it to come near us. Psalm 91 reiterates this theme: "Evil can't get close to you, harm can't get through the door." (MSG) We will never know how many times our heavenly Father has stopped harm at the door of our lives.

But the second way that God protects us is sometimes harder to understand. Sometimes God protects us *in* trouble. Sometimes He allows circumstances to come into our lives that we don't understand. Sickness or conflict or bad situations enter our world and we wonder if God has somehow forgotten to be our protector. But the truth is that God *is still* our protector. He doesn't always stop the trouble before it comes to us, but He is *always* there with us and has His hand on us during the trial. Psalm 91:15 says, "When they call on me, I will be with them in trouble. I will rescue them and honor them." You notice that this scripture doesn't say, "They will never be in trouble ..." but instead is says that when we are *in* the trouble, He will be our rescuer; He is at work through the fire or the storm or whatever it is we are facing.

We might wonder, "God, why did you allow this to happen to me?" The unfortunate reality is that we don't get to choose which times God keeps us *from* trouble and which times He keeps us *during* the trial. I don't always understand why – but I have experienced over and over the absolute truth that He faithfully is guarding me even in the midst of a storm.

My dear friend Arvilla and her husband were hit head on by a drunk driver 13 years ago. Arvilla sustained an incredible amount of injury and countless surgeries on her face to repair the damage caused by the accident. Now, I am confident that God could have stopped that driver from getting into his car that night, but He didn't. I am also confident that Arvilla could have died that day, but God protected her life during the horrible trauma. She was in the Father's hand throughout the accident, and the aftermath of that life-altering event. Through her experience, she was able to be a witness to countless people, including the very man who hit her. During his trial, she and her husband were able to offer him forgiveness because of the love of Jesus in their hearts. She has shared her testimony with countless others and is an example to many that Jesus is indeed our healer, restorer and protector.

I think sometimes when I am in the midst of a storm, I get frustrated that God didn't keep me from the trial, and I miss the comfort that comes in knowing that He is walking with me in the midst of it. Instead of getting bitter and angry at God, we should throw all of our questions at His feet and say, "I'm not sure what You're doing here, God, but please be with me as I go through this trial. Redeem it for good. Let me learn through it. I know I can get through anything with your help."

Isaiah 25:4 says, "But to the poor, O Lord, you are a refuge from the storm. To the needy in distress, you're a shelter from the rain and the heat." When we are in the midst of a storm, there is no greater shelter than in the arms of our Father.

Every year we have little bunnies that like to come into our backyard to make a home. These are not your average, run-of-the-mill bunnies, these are bunnies with guts. Not only do I have four kids running around like crazy people, I also have a wild beagle that loves a good chase. These bunnies have some nerve: Every year I see them make a home underneath our kids' play set. They find a spot that has long grass, a roof over their head, and shelter from the elements. When it rains, they hide underneath the wooden structure and escape the storm.

No matter what situation in which you find yourself, God the Father desires to be your shelter. He wants to be the place where you hide yourself and find refuge during the storm. We can know that we will find safety and protection in the midst of anything we may face.

You and I should be secure in the fact that God is always protecting us. Jeremiah 15:19 says, "They will fight against you like an attacking army, but I will make you as secure as a fortified wall. They will not conquer you, for I will protect and deliver you. I, the Lord have spoken. Yes, I will certainly keep you safe from these wicked men. I will rescue them from their cruel hands."

So, how should the knowledge that God is protecting us affect our lives? First of all, we should not be fearful. We should not fret or worry about situations, whether they are real or imagined. Knowing that God is our shield and fortress should quiet and calm our worry and anxiety. Psalm 113:6-7 describes a person who is confident in God as their protector. It says, "Such people will not be overcome by evil circumstances. Those who are righteous will be long remembered. They do not fear bad news; they confidently trust the Lord to care for them."

Secondly, when we understand that God is watching over us, we should have peace. There should be a sense of calm that surrounds us. We should not be constantly allowing our minds to take us to the "worst-case scenario" and allowing ourselves to be anxious and full of fear.

A few years ago, Jeff was off with some friends for the evening, and I decided that is was time to clean out my basement. So, I put the kids to bed upstairs and proceeded down into my messy storage room to sort through all of our junk. About an hour into my project, I thought I heard Jeff come home. I heard the garage door open and footsteps move across the floor above me. I came upstairs to talk to Jeff, but Jeff was nowhere to be found. I walked throughout the house, but I couldn't find him. I finally went to the garage and opened the door to see that his car was not there; I instantly felt my stomach drop and a lump fill my throat.

Was there someone in my house? I could have sworn that I heard footsteps. I ran upstairs to check on my kids as my heart pounded faster and faster in my chest. My hands were shaking as I went to each of their rooms and checked behind the doors and in the closets whispering prayers the entire time. Suddenly, I heard a door slam downstairs and Jeff's voice call my name.

An enormous wave of relief swept over me and I felt my fears immediately subside. Now, the ironic thing is that I still didn't know if someone was in my house or not. And although he is quite a man, I'm not sure what Jeff would have done if there actually had been someone there. But just knowing that he was *there* completely eased my fear; it was as if suddenly the burden was not my own to carry, but I knew that Jeff would carry it for me. I wasn't left to face the danger alone; I knew that my husband would take care of me and our children.

The instant feeling of relief that I just described is how

peace feels. It is the calm that comes over you when you realize that you are not alone. Knowing that there is someone there who is going to protect you and keep you safe. The peace you and I have in our hearts should cause all anxiety, fret and worry to subside. Psalm 3:5 says, "I lay down and slept. I woke up in safety, for the Lord was watching over me. I am not afraid of ten thousand enemies who surround me on every side."

Yes, there are things to fear in this life. There are bad events and bad people, but God has promised us that He will always be with us. I tell my kids all the time, "You don't have to be afraid of anything, because God is always with you." We are never alone; we don't have to fear what may come our way because we know that whatever we may face, God is there, protecting us. We should embrace His watch over us, and run to Him whenever we find ourselves fearful.

And lastly, the knowledge that God is our protector should make us feel cared for and treasured. When we think back to our earlier list about why a woman wants to feel protected, we remember that a woman wants to feel protected because it is a demonstration of someone's love for her. Watching over us is yet another way that God expresses His amazing love for you and for me. Because you are so important and valuable to Him, He stands before you as a refuge and shield of protection.

I love this verse in Zephaniah 3:16-17. It says, " Cheer up, Zion! Don't be afraid! For the Lord your God is living among you. He is a mighty savior. He will take delight in you with gladness. With His love, He will calm all your fears."

CHAPTER 9

THE FATHER'S LOVE

So here we are - at the heart of the issue; at the crux of the matter; the place where it all begins and ends. I have to be honest - I have started to write this chapter over and over and over again. I have read, studied and pondered the idea of how much God loves me. I want to somehow be able to pen the words that will open your eyes to the amazing love that God the Father has for you, but my words seem to fall short.

The whole inspiration behind this book was the many, many conversations that I have had with women over the years concerning the love of God. It was always amazing to me how many women don't *really* believe that God loves them - we don't *really* understand His great affection for us... and we *really* don't think His love is given to us unconditionally – we think we need to earn it.

As I sought to minister the truth of God's love to women, I was faced with a sobering fact: I couldn't write about it, because *I* didn't believe it. Oops.

I even taught this lesson at a Bible study and decided to "focus on the facts." I told the ladies that we need to just remind ourselves that God DOES love us, and focus on the scriptures that tell us so; I explained that we may never understand it, but that is what faith is all about.

Now those sentiments are true - there is a part of us that must believe what we cannot feel. There is an element of faith to our understanding of God's love and it's important that we don't let our emotions rob us of the truth.

But something in my heart ached a little as I shared those words. Yes, I know that God loves me, but I wanted to *know* that God loves me. I knew there had to be more than just a "will-based acceptance" of God's heart for me. That certainly can't be the kind of relationship that God was interested in having with me.

It would be as if I kept my marriage certificate framed on a wall in my kitchen so that I could remind myself that Jeff loved me. I could tell myself, "Well, he's legally required to be here, so he must love me. He signed the papers, he said the vows, so that's all there is to it." What if the core of my marriage was a cold set of facts left to convince my heart that this man did indeed love me?

As a woman, there's no way that would be enough: We want to *feel* loved. We want to have special, intimate ways in which our loved one pours out his heart to us; we want to be adored, cherished, understood and accepted. Something in me needs to feel it; I need to hear it; I need to experience it; I need to feel it from my husband … and I need to feel it from God.

Truth be told, I have spent many years feeling sheepish about the fact that I want to "feel" loved. I think, "Don't be so silly, Kristie. You're just being high maintenance - you don't have any reason *not* to believe, so why do you need the constant affirmation?" I have been embarrassed by the side of me that longs for an emotional connection to God; the parts of me that want to go past the intellectual theology and feel the supernatural embrace of my Heavenly Father. But I'm starting to understand that although there are times when I need to believe based on faith and intellect, that it's okay for me to need to connect to God emotionally as well. I am starting to embrace the way God made me - I believe that God has put that longing in my heart for a reason; He created me with an ache that can only be filled by the love only He can offer.

There is a common thread in all of us that hungers for love, acceptance and affection. And as women, it seems that our need for an emotional connection to a loving God seems even more vital. My friend Lindsay Willis says, "God wired women this way: We love best when we are responding to love." When I am confident of God's love for me everything else seems to fall into place.

I am beginning to realize how many years I have spent seeking to have that longing fulfilled by other people - friends, family, husband, kids, other people's praise, other people's acceptance ... the list is immeasurable. That need to feel loved seems unquenchable in me and I have spent years looking everywhere possible to have it met.

I have amazingly loving parents who affirmed and loved me without condition ... but I still needed more. I found a husband who adores and cherishes me every day ... but it's still not enough. I have four children who depend on me in every way imaginable, and yet I still long for significance. Every victory, every accomplishment, every round of applause has only been a drop in the deep ocean of longing that my heart holds.

Will there ever be enough? Is there a love that can quench my thirst? Can an invisible God reveal Himself to me tangibly and satisfy the need of my heart?

The answer is a resounding YES! The Bible is full of scriptures that describe the grandness of the Father's love. He tells us that it is higher than the heavens; He tells us there is nothing in heaven or earth that can ever separate us from it; He says He wants to lavishly pour out His love on us in immeasurable ways.

I believe the Father delights in revealing His love for us. It's like Christmas morning for Him. Here we are, his daughters, searching, lonely and in need. So He places a beautifully wrapped gift before us - He knows that inside lies the treasure that will satisfy the longing. Imagine the anticipation He feels in knowing we are about to possess the very thing that will bring us the fullness of life of which we are in desperate need.

But for most of us we fail to open the gift. We look at Him and say, "You probably don't want to give this to *me*." We bow our heads in shame and reply, "You know the things I've done … I don't deserve this." Or we think, "Hang on … let me go do some more stuff for you, and *then* I'll be worthy to open it up."

Instead of receiving the beautiful gift of His love we walk

away; the longing in our hearts grows deeper and the ache grows wider and we wonder why we don't "feel" His love. It's not that He hasn't offered it, we haven't *accepted* it.

Why do we do that? Why do we assume that God's love isn't what He says it is? Why don't we believe He truly wants to offer *us* His love free of charge?

I think we forget that God's love is not the same as human love: Human love can walk away; human love can fade and flicker; human love rides waves of intensity; human love is always conditional.

Even the greatest earthly love has human reactions and emotions to deal with. We have our own needs, insecurities, shortcomings and failures that taint our relationships; the purist earthly love will still be subject to our broken nature.

The love I have for my children is about as pure a love as I know - they are my heart and soul. I cannot imagine anything that would ever cause me to love them any less than I do right now. And every day, I see my heart for them deepen and grow. But I fail them: I get angry at the things they do; I overreact to situations and say things I wish I hadn't said; I get selfish and frustrated when I want time to myself. My love for them is not strong enough to keep me from making mistakes; my love for them cannot erase my humanness - no matter how much I adore them, I am still going to let them down.

But God is perfect - His love never changes. It is exactly the same the day you do a selfless good deed, as it is the day you commit a selfish sin. His love is equal in the moments you are seeking Him and the moments you are defiantly walking away.

God is not prone to human emotion: He doesn't get tired and wish you would just give him a break; He doesn't react in frustration and regret it later; His needs never get in the way of His love because He is complete and whole in Himself.

Therefore, His love is the only truly pure love - it is given without condition. It endures unchanged regardless of our responses ... it is offered freely – there is nothing you can do to earn it.

But most of us put the conditions and characteristics that we are used to in our human relationships onto our Heavenly Father. We decide that He must be tired of our shortcomings. We think we need to do more in order to gain His affection and we fail to recognize the abundance of what He is offering us.

This has been a very personal journey for me over the last few years. I knew in my head that God loved me; I told others that God loved them; I sang about it, taught about it and shared it with everyone I could. Ironically, I was confident that God loved YOU, but somewhere deep in my heart, I was not sure of it for me.

I have been a Christian since I was five years old. I was sitting in the balcony of the church on a Sunday night and listened to the pastor talk about what Jesus had done for me on the cross. He said that because I was human and sinful, that I was separated from God. There was nothing I could do to earn salvation. But when Jesus died on the cross, He made a way for me to have a relationship with God. If I asked Jesus to come into my heart, then He would come and live in me forever. That night, I received the gift of salvation. I made a decision to accept God's grace and let Him have control of my life. And I have faithfully followed Jesus from that day forward.

I truly believe that God is my Savior. I have complete assurance that I am going to heaven. I committed my life to Him and have been on a journey of walking out my salvation for thirty years.

But what I had begun to realize, was that somewhere along the way, I allowed myself to believe that God's *love* for me was based upon my behavior. I convinced myself that the more I did for God, the more He would love me - instead of serving Him out of the depths of our relationship, I was trying to earn His love by doing more and being better ... and I was tired. I felt like I was on a giant hamster wheel of trying to be better and do more and sin less and work harder. I felt that ache in my heart growing deeper and deeper, so I worked harder and harder trying to earn God's approval. My efforts were not producing any greater revelation of love, and were simply wearing me out.

One night after a church service, I went to a dear friend and slumped down in the seat next to her ... I was at my end. I felt so far away from God; It seemed as if I was knocking at the door to His heart, and He was nowhere to be found. As I talked and prayed with her, we began discussing what was going on in my heart.

"I'm trying so hard!" I cried out to my friend. "I don't

know what else He wants from me." I realized the depths of my disappointment in myself for being unable to rise to the standard required in my mind; I realized the frustration I had towards Him for my perception that He was the one withholding His love until I could do better.

My friend gently began to ask me some questions. "Who would you be if you weren't a pastor's wife, Kristie?" I had no answer. "Who would you be if you weren't a teacher or a singer?" My mind was blank. "What if you never did another thing *for* God? Would he still love you?" I didn't know.

"Kristie," my friend whispered, "you don't have to do anything for Him." Hot tears began to pour down my face and I forced myself to digest the words she was saying to me. "You don't have to *be* anything; you don't have to *do* anything else, ever again - He just wants you to be his daughter … that's it."

Romans 8:15 says, "So you should not be like cowering fearful slaves. You should behave instead like God's own children, adopted into His family – calling Him "Father, dear Father."

Years and years of service based on the notion that I had to earn God's favor had left me as "a cowering, fearful slave." My relationship with Him was all about duty and obligation. And deep down, I had gotten tired - I had become resentful; I was weary; I had forgotten that I was His daughter.

Imagine if Lucy had decided that Jeff and I only wanted her in our lives to help out around the house. If our only interest in her was what she could give. "Lucy! How many loads of laundry did you get done today?" "Lucy! How many hours did you watch your brother and sisters?" "Lucy! When are you going to finish dinner?" How long would she enjoy our home and our relationship? Not long.

Jeff's relationship with Lucy has nothing to do with what she gives him. He doesn't love her based on what she does or doesn't do. How silly to think that we could love our children more or less based on how much they "do" for us.

And yet, I have allowed myself to think this way about God. Invite a friend to church; a point on the love chart for me. Volunteer in the nursery; earn another point. Don't cheat on my taxes; point. Be a good wife, mother, and friend; point, point, point. But forget to read my Bible; loose a point. Act out in anger; loose a point. Don't serve, don't give, don't pray; loose, loose, loose.

What does this kind of understanding of God do to our relationship with Him? It turns us into "fearful cowering slaves." Our relationship becomes not about affection and devotion, but one based on fear and uncertainty. It may not start out that way, but give it enough time on the "point" system, and it will definitely turn that way.

What God really desires is for us to be His daughters. That we would learn to receive the love that He is offering to us - a love that cannot be earned and cannot be lost. He wants us to stop trying to deserve it and simply open up the package.

I made a choice that night sitting in the darkened church with my friend: I decided to get off the wheel. I determined in my heart that I was going to accept God's love for me for exactly what it was. I was going to lay down all the veiled perceptions that I had accumulated along the way, and instead receive the gift that He was offering me.

As I have laid aside the idea that I have to earn the Father's affection, I have felt the ache in my heart begin to subside.

The best word I can use to describe my new understanding of God's love for me is this: Easy. Instead of feeling like I am trying to earn His love, I am sitting back and watching Him reveal it to me in ways I never imagined. Whereas before I was riding the wave of uncertainty in my relationship with God, now I find myself secure in His affection for me and at rest in my relationship with Him.

I told you earlier that there is something inside of me that needs to "feel" loved. The truth is, my distorted view of trying to earn God's approval blinded me to the ways He was demonstrating His love to me everyday. Putting the responsibility in my hands to manufacture His love had robbed me of the truth that He was daily offering me all the affection I could ever long for.

And He is offering it to you too - His love is right there, waiting for you to reach out and take it. The part of you that desires to feel His love can be filled to overflowing. He longs to flood your heart with His goodness and kindness. He doesn't want a slave, He wants a *daughter*.

As I have embraced the love God has for me, I have gained a better understanding of what God *really* wants from me: He wants me to love Him back; He wants me to partner with Him in telling others about His love; He wants me to invest in my relationship with Him, and everything else flows out of that. I am doing just as much in service to God as I was before, but instead of doing it *for* Him, I am doing it *with* Him … there is a huge difference.

His discipline isn't scary anymore. It's not easy, but I trust it. His challenges are still intimidating, but I know He is the one who can give me strength. The fears of this world still creep in, but I know that if I run into His arms, I will find comfort and protection. I still have my moments of insecurity and trying to earn His favor, but He gently leads me back to that place of rest and ease in Him. And He wants the same thing for you.

God the Father is sitting right in front of you, holding out the gift of His love, and He is waiting for you to open it. When you lay aside all your doubts and rip open the package, you will forever be changed.

My sweet friends, open up your hearts and receive what the Father is offering you. Believe that *it is for YOU*. Not for everyone else, not for "someday when you've got your act together," but for right now. For this very moment. For you.

And I pray that you, being rooted and established in love, will have the power, together with all the saints, to grasp how wide and long and high and deep is the love of Christ, and to know this love that surpasses knowledge - that you may be filled to the measure of the fullness of God. (Ephesians 3:17-19 NIV)